The
FRIENDSHIP
BOOK

of Francis Gay

D. C. THOMSON & CO., LTD.
London Glasgow Manchester Dundee
ISBN 0-85116-459-5

A Thought
For Each Day
In 1990

There are no strangers —
just friends who have never met.

ALWAYS ANOTHER DAY

We can't all follow the eagle
And soar to a distant crag,
And though our hearts are willing,
The pace at times may flag.
Why should we rush to climb each hill?
Tomorrow they'll be with us still.

JANUARY

MONDAY—JANUARY 1.

AS one year gives way to another, it is inevitable that our minds turn to that mysterious subject we call "time". Some of our thoughts and sayings about it seem to have a rather gloomy aspect to them — "Time flies," we say, for example. Ben Jonson called time "that old bald cheater", while another poet spoke of "Time's devouring hand". Not the most cheerful thoughts for the end of a year!

Thank goodness, there is another side to all this. A Danish saying claims, "Time cures more than the doctor", while the Germans have a proverb "Time brings roses". Then there is "Time the great discoverer", "The grand instructor, Time", "Time, an endless song", and, best of all, perhaps, "There's a good time coming"! So, we leave one year and greet another. A Happy New Year to you!

TUESDAY—JANUARY 2.

I WAS enjoying a cup of tea with my friend Mary the other day when we were disturbed by a bit of a commotion outside.

Looking out of the window, we could see two youngsters having a tiff on their way home from school. To make matters worse, the two mothers appeared on the scene and exchanged heated words before each marched off with her own offspring.

"Oh, what a pity that had to happen," said Mary, shaking her head sadly. "Speak when you're angry and you'll make the best speech you'll ever regret."

It was a quaint way of putting it, perhaps — but I know exactly what she meant.

THE FRIENDSHIP BOOK

THE Lady of the House was smiling yesterday after she had paid the milkman. He is a cheerful character, and he told her of a delightful note left him by a customer. It read: "Please ask your cows to produce an extra pint every day until further notice".

He told the Lady of the House the customer was quite right — she was giving credit where it belonged — and he'd had a word with his cows and they couldn't see any problem in fulfilling the request!

LET go of the old,
Reach out for the new,
For the past is cold,
And the future is due;
Each year holds memories,
Some happy — some sad,
We must treasure the good,
Let go of the bad;
Make the most of each day,
At work and at play,
For the old year is history,
The future — a mystery.
Phyllis Ellison.

THE art of leadership was once convincingly demonstrated to a group of young officers by General Dwight D. Eisenhower, later to become President of the United States.

Placing a piece of string on the table, he said, "Pull it — and it will follow you anywhere. Shove it — and it will go nowhere at all."

SATURDAY—JANUARY 6.

THE organist and Master of Music at St. Thomas's School in Leipzig, played a few chords and improvised. He paused to jot down the notes. It was not always easy to compose a fresh piece of music for the boys every Sunday, yet that was the condition of his employment.

So Johann Sebastian Bach worked hard. He expected that nobody, apart from the choir boys and the small congregation, would ever hear his compositions, but that did not matter to him. He lived and breathed music; nothing gave him greater pleasure than composing and playing.

Even when he became well-known in later years, he never imagined that his 265 church cantatas, 263 chorals, 14 larger works and 365 organ compositions would become world famous. Some of his compositions are better known than others; for example, St Matthew's Passion. Even people who do not know much about music are sure to be aware of two favourites — "Jesu, Joy of Man's Desiring" and "Sheep May Safely Graze", two of the most beautiful pieces of church music ever composed.

Everything he wrote was written to the best of his ability. That is probably why, in our own times, Ralph Vaughan Williams maintained that Bach's music was "something for all time". It inspired him as it inspires us all.

SUNDAY—JANUARY 7.

BUT the hour cometh, and now is, when the true worshippers shall worship the Father in spirit and in truth; for the Father seeketh such to worship him.
John 4:23

HIDDEN VALLEY

THE FRIENDSHIP BOOK

WHEN Gran and Grandpa had left for home, many miles away, after a wonderful Christmas with their family, the house seemed very empty to three-year-old Peter. Then when the tree was taken down it was just too much.

"Where are Gran and Grandpa, Mummy?" he kept asking. "Where has Christmas gone?"

Was this just a question from a puzzled little boy or do you think there might be a little more to it?

Christmas brings out the best in us all. How marvellous it would be, when the parties are over and the lights have been put away, if we could keep some of that good cheer which warmed our hearts at the festive season for the ordinary days ahead.

Then Christmas wouldn't have "gone" anywhere!

"WHAT is knowledge?" someone once asked Confucius, the great Chinese philosopher.

"Knowing people," was the reply.

"And what is humanity?" asked his questioner.

"Loving people," answered the great man.

Simple, isn't it?

I LIKE the story I heard about the boy who came home from school and announced that there was a new little girl in his class and that she was Indian.

"And does she speak English?" asked his mother.

"No, not yet," he replied, "but it doesn't matter because she laughs in English."

We can usually rely on a child to keep to the essentials!

THE FRIENDSHIP BOOK

WHEN we visited our old friend Mary just before New Year we found that she had two calendars hung side by side. They were the "tear-off" type, one page allocated to each day, with the date in a large red figure and then several lines of print in black at the bottom.

Mary smiled when she saw me glancing at them. "You think they're both alike, don't you, Francis?"

"Well, yes," I admitted.

"You'd better look at them a bit more closely," she replied.

When I did so, I found that one had "A Joke for the Day" and the other "A Text for the Day".

Can you think of any better way of starting each morning — with a smile *and* a text! I think Mary is going to have a very happy year.

IN her short life, Winifred Holtby made her name as a brilliant writer. But it was not only her literary achievements that made people proud to have known her, for she was one of those people who gave all who knew her the uplifting feeling that the world was a happier place simply because she was there.

It was said that she was always kind and gentle, with a smile for everyone. Phyllis Bentley, the Yorkshire novelist, wrote: "She was the best person I have ever known. When she entered the room it felt as if all the lights had been turned up to blaze higher."

Winifred Holtby was one of life's "golden girls" and of course we can't all possess her gift to the same degree. Isn't it a sobering thought, though, that the way we do something can either darken someone else's day — or brighten it up?

SATURDAY—JANUARY 13.

LITTLE ROY was the son of the stationmaster at Mount Clemens, near Detroit. One day he was playing at a siding when a freight wagon came rolling along the line. Roy was right in its path.

A teenager on the platform rushed to the rescue and snatched Roy to safety just in time. Afterwards, the stationmaster asked the youth if there was anything he could do to repay him for saving his son's life.

"Could you teach me telegraphy?" the young man asked eagerly. Within four months he had mastered it, and the grateful stationmaster was later to recommend him for the job of telegraph operator on the Grand Trunk Line.

So began the astonishing career of Thomas Alva Edison, who perfected the incandescent electric lamp, the dynamo, and many other things, but who is perhaps best known for his famous saying: "Genius is one per cent. inspiration — and ninety-nine per cent. perspiration".

SUNDAY—JANUARY 14.

AND hope maketh not ashamed; because the love of God is shed abroad in our hearts by the Holy Ghost which is given unto us.   Romans 5:5

MONDAY—JANUARY 15.

I CAME across this passage recently. I don't know who wrote it, but it strikes me as being full of truth:

"In the heart of every Winter is a quivering Spring, and behind the veil of each night there is a smiling dawn."

B

TUESDAY—JANUARY 16.

ERIC LIDDELL, the 1924 Olympic Games Gold Medallist, died in a Japanese prisoner-of-war camp in 1945. The man who was to become the inspiration for the film "Chariots of Fire" had gone as a Christian teacher to Asia in 1925. It is said that he often regarded himself as a failure.

Towards the end of his life, the famous writer Sir Rider Haggard began to fear that he, too, had not been really successful. Yet, in addition to being an internationally-known author, he had campaigned long and successfully for many good causes.

Someone else in far different circumstances who came to regard his life as a failure was Mozart. Desperately ill and poor, he continued to complete his "Requiem", even though he had little hope of its success. It was to become one of his most famous compositions — after his death.

Someone once wrote: "The fear of failing divides success and failure rigidly — for who can say where success ends and failure begins?"

Perhaps, after all, there is only one real failure in life — when you stop trying.

WEDNESDAY—JANUARY 17.

RECENTLY in church we sang John Greenleaf Whittier's hymn which contains the words, "I know not what the future hath of marvel or surprise . . ."

I couldn't help thinking what a wonderful philosophy of life that is, especially at the beginning of a New Year. So often, when we contemplate the future, it is with a certain amount of foreboding and we dread "what a day may bring forth".

Not so Whittier. He looks for marvel, surprise, wonder, miracle.

THE FRIENDSHIP BOOK

YOUNG Stevie was off school, recovering from a sore throat. When I called in, he was deep in thought, puzzling over a jig-saw. Only three pieces were left to fit in at the bottom left-hand corner.

"They just won't go!" he exclaimed in annoyance. Then his face cleared. "Gosh, I've had them in the wrong order all the time. Look!" And in seconds, with a quick re-arrangement, the picture was complete.

He grinned. "Easy, wasn't it, after all?"

I felt that Stevie had learned a valuable lesson. A lot of life's problem pieces seem hard to fit together, but if we look at them the right way round, we're on our way to working out the complete pattern.

FRIDAY—JANUARY 19.

THE rain was lashing down when the Lady of the House arrived home windswept and drenched after a visit to a friend one evening, recently.

When I remarked on the unpleasant journey home she must have had, she surprised me by saying she had hardly noticed the weather! She said she'd been too busy thinking back over the enjoyable hour she'd spent with her friend.

Such is the quality of real friendship. It doesn't depend on fair weather and clear blue skies for survival. A good friendship can endure, no matter how severe the tests.

SATURDAY—JANUARY 20.

MY mother often used to quote this old proverb: "If you live in Grumble Row, flit into Thanksgiving Street."

There a lot of sense in it, isn't there?

SUNDAY—JANUARY 21.

I THANK my God upon every remembrance of you,
Always in every prayer of mine for you all making request with joy,
For your fellowship in the gospel from the first day until now.   Philippians 1: 3-5

MONDAY—JANUARY 22.

VISITORS to Knutsford, the charming old Cheshire town portrayed as "Cranford" by Elizabeth Cleghorn Gaskell, often call at the 17th century Brook Street Unitarian Chapel which has close links with her and her family. Here they can see her grave.

Unlike many authors who become famous in adult life, writing does not appear to have been one of Elizabeth's childhood interests. It was only after the death of her baby son that her husband, the Rev. William Gaskell, a Unitarian minister in Manchester, suggested that she should write a book to take her mind off the sorrow.

She began "Mary Barton", a story of 19th century industrial life. Through her characters and situations shone Mrs Gaskell's sympathy with the poor and under-privileged workers in the north of England, for she knew the conditions under which they lived and worked. The novel was published in 1848 and was widely-read.

Through all the ups and downs of being a minister's wife, she was staunchly supported by her husband, William, without whose sympathetic help she would probably never have become the famous author she did.

THE MESSAGE

Remember, as the rockets soar and golden showers fall,
God lit a single star to bring the gladdest news of all.

THE FRIENDSHIP BOOK

AS I was walking through my garden on a cold January day, I noticed that the snowdrops were already showing their brave white bells. It won't be long before the whole garden bursts into life again with a glorious array of Spring flowers.

I read recently, "A really successful garden is made of a happy balance of shrubs, perennials, annuals and bulbs." It made me think about life in general and the necessity to keep a proper balance — between work and play, activity and rest, giving and receiving, care for ourselves and concern for others. To live with each area complementing the others must surely result in harmony and happiness for ourselves and for those around us.

JOSEPH ADDISON, hymn writer and one-time editor of "The Spectator", gave this sound advice:
"If you wish success in life, make Perseverance your bosom friend, Experience your wise counsellor, Caution your elder brother, and Hope your guardian genius."

These would be Good Companions indeed!

MY young neighbour Billy loves to catch me out with his riddles.

"Mr Gay," he called over the garden wall, "do you know what happened to the two kangaroos that got married?"

"No, I can't answer that one," I said.

"Why, they lived *hoppily* ever after," chuckled Billy, skipping off.

THE FRIENDSHIP BOOK

MRS SANDERS of Rustington, Sussex, tells me a friend in Australia sent her this verse. Old age, it seems, feels the same the whole world over!

When I was young, my shoes were red,
I could kick my heels right over my head.
As I grew older, my shoes were blue,
But still I could dance the whole night through.
Now that I'm old, my shoes are black,
I walk to the store and then puff back.
I get up each morning and dust off my wits,
Pick up the paper and read the "obits",
If my name's not there, I know I'm not dead,
So I take a good breakfast and go back to bed.

I MET little Jenny coming home from school the other day and asked her what she had been doing.

"We tied our shoelaces," she said.

I thought there was nothing remarkable in this, but she surprised me: "We had to do it with only one hand."

Computer games and modern maths I'd heard about, but this was a new skill! I asked her how she'd got on.

"It was hopeless until our teacher told us how it's done."

I wanted to know that myself and I listened carefully as Jenny continued, "She said we wouldn't manage it on our own, but if we got together in pairs then we'd all have two hands. We did — and it was easy!"

Jenny ran off to play and I was left smiling to myself. What a lovely way to learn that "a trouble shared is a trouble halved!"

THE FRIENDSHIP BOOK

SUNDAY—JANUARY 28.

LET your speech be alway with grace, seasoned with salt, that ye may know how ye ought to answer every man.   Colossians 4:6

MONDAY—JANUARY 29.

VISITORS to lovely Robin Hood's Bay, situated between Scarborough and Whitby, may notice a plaque outside a cottage where in earlier times lived a little boy who became a writer and put his village on the literary map as Bramblewick.

As a child, Leo Walmsley spent hours watching the fishermen of Bay, as this village is affectionately known. He grew older and nothing delighted him more than to accompany the fishermen on their expeditions.

Nothing outstanding about that, you might say. After all, lots of boys in numerous fishing villages have done the same. Few, however, have made their villages as famous as Leo Walmsley was to do with such novels as "Three Fevers", "Phantom Lobster", "Foreigners", "Sally Lunn" and autobiographical works such as "Love In The Sun" and the later "Paradise Creek". All were set in the "Bramblewick" area and later around Fowey, Cornwall. Fame came to him when he wrote about the life and events he knew and loved.

In May 1985, a Leo Walmsley Society was formed, not merely to admire his books, but also to preserve memories of the man who was never wittingly known to say an unkind word or do an unkind action to anyone. He is remembered as one who always went out of his way to help others.

<u>TUESDAY—JANUARY 30.</u>

GEORGE, a farm worker, had got into the habit of not turning up on Monday mornings. This irritated the farmer, so one day he decided to have a word with him.

"Now look here, George," he said, "this habit of taking Mondays off has to stop. You'll have to change your ways."

The following Monday morning, George reported for work, but on Tuesday he was missing again. The farmer was furious. "What's the meaning of this?" he demanded. "I thought you'd agreed to change your ways."

"Oh, I'm sorry, sir," replied George, "I thought you said 'change your days'!"

<u>WEDNESDAY—JANUARY 31.</u>

I CAME across this old traditional blessing recently. It's intended for what most of us value above all other things — our home:

> *Touch the lintel and touch the wall,*
> *Nothing but blessing here befall!*
> *Bless the candle that stands by itself,*
> *Bless the books on the mantelshelf,*
> *Bless the hearth and the light it sheds,*
> *Bless the pillow for tired heads.*
> *Those who tarry here, let them know*
> *A threefold blessing before they go:*
> *Sleep for weariness — peace for sorrow —*
> *Faith in yesterday and tomorrow.*
> *Those who go from here, let them bear*
> *The blessing of hope wherever they fare.*
> *Lintel and window, sill and wall,*
> *Nothing but good this place befall.*

 # FEBRUARY

THURSDAY—FEBRUARY 1.

RECENTLY some friends of ours were moving house and the Lady of the House and I spent the day with them trying to help to bring order out of chaos.

I was reminded of a television programme I saw some time ago about a day in the life of a removal man. Towards the end of the programme, with the last piece of furniture in place, he put a clock on the mantelpiece, set it going and listened to it striking. "There," he said, "now life is back in the house! That makes it a home!"

I had never really thought about it like that before, but it's true, isn't it? The chiming and ticking of a clock is part of the life of our homes, keeping us company and reminding us, each in its own friendly way, of the good things to come.

FRIDAY—FEBRUARY 2.

WHAT lovely, unexpected things are to be found in the countryside!

I remember, on a bitterly cold February day, I once went for a walk in Milldale, one of Derbyshire's most beautiful valleys. Following the curve of the River Dove, I came suddenly upon a hillside of wild snowdrops stretching as far as the eye could see. Their loveliness was breathtaking and I stood for some time, just staring in wonder.

I learned later that in flower language the snowdrop means hope, and indeed when we see these first delicate flowers of the New Year we are filled with the hope that Spring is not far away.

SATURDAY—FEBRUARY 3.

THIS lovely mother's prayer is by D. J. Morris of Stockton-on-the-Forest, York:

Watch over her, Lord,
That child that I love,
Watch over her, Lord,
From your heaven above.
Keep her from suffering,
Loved let her be,
Watch over her, Lord,
As you've watched over me.

SUNDAY—FEBRUARY 4.

BLESSED is the man that endureth temptation: for when he is tried, he shall receive the crown of life, which the Lord hath promised to them that love him.

James 1:12

MONDAY—FEBRUARY 5.

FOR many years, J. B. Priestley was one of the foremost English writers, with a vast output of thought-provoking novels, plays and essays. As an old man, in the last chapter of his autobiography, he had this to say:

"I don't know how I stand with the general public, but among my family and friends I have a solid, dark reputation as an inveterate grumbler. However, whatever may be said to the contrary, I don't grumble for grumbling's sake . . . I realise that I have had more luck than I ever deserved to have. It is time, before it is too late, that I gave the world more smiles and far fewer scowls, and began thanking God on my knees."

A good philosophy indeed!

PERSEVERANCE

Successes can be measured
In varying amounts.
So long as we're still trying —
That's the thing that counts.
Feeling sure, each bright new day
Something good is on its way.

THE FRIENDSHIP BOOK

DO you know what the three C's are? They are Courage, Compassion and Concern and we need them all as we go through life.

We would be lost without courage — not only physical bravery, but the ability to stand up for what is right and true. It is so easy to float with the stream of public opinion no matter how wrong we think it to be. When gossip is repeated, it takes courage to stem the flow and to believe the best of everyone.

Compassion — how valuable that is! We can bring consolation to the sufferer, comfort to the bereaved, the sick and unfortunate.

All great men and women who have helped to make life better for others have been motivated by compassion and it has led them to the third "C" — concern.

It was genuine concern that prompted the great reformers of earlier times. There are similar people today working for the poor and deprived. In our own small way we can help them — if we care enough.

I'M sure many of us have a "down" day from time to time and I'm passing on these anonymous lines entitled "Faith" in the hope that they may be a comfort next time *you* feel depressed:

> *Doubt sees the obstacles,*
>   *Faith sees the way.*
> *Doubt sees the darkest night,*
>   *Faith sees the day.*
> *Doubt dreads to take a step,*
>   *Faith soars on high.*
> *Doubt whispers, "Who believes?"*
>   *Faith answers "I".*

Thursday—February 8.

THE delicate snowdrop, symbol of purity and dedicated to the Virgin Mary, can often be found in our gardens when Winter is at its most severe. In fact, the French name for it means "snow piercer". German people called it *Schneeglöckchen* or little snowbell and have this delightful story about its origin:

When God created heaven and earth, everything was given a beautiful colour — gold for the sun, silver for the stars, blue for the sky, green for the trees, and so on. As the snow waited patiently for his colour, he found that nothing was left for him and he was sad because he thought nobody would notice him. So the Creator asked the rainbow-coloured flowers if they could spare some colour, but they all refused — all except the little white snowdrop.

"You can have my colour gladly," she said. So the snow accepted it happily, and in gratitude, it is said, he promised that whenever Winter came, he would cover the snowdrop with a warm blanket to protect it from the frost.

Friday—February 9.

I WAS listening to a young author describing what he believed to be the secret of living to a ripe old age and enjoying doing so. These were his suggestions:

Walk a lot.

Keep your sense of humour.

Don't hark back to the past, but treat each day as a new adventure.

I am sure the recipe is one hundred per cent correct. And even if it's not exactly new, it's pleasant to see a new generation rediscovering old truths!

SATURDAY—FEBRUARY 10.

" A GOOD laugh is sunshine in a house", said the author W.M. Thackeray, while S. Chamfort wrote, "The most useless day of all is that in which we have not laughed". The poet John Betjeman spoke of "the bonus of laughter", while Robert Louis Stevenson said, "That people should learn to laugh is a better preparation for life than many things higher and better sounding in the world's ear".

The 17th century writer, Matthew Green, penned the phrase "laugh and grow well", a view that has gained support from a number of modern medical authorities.

In view of this collected wisdom, I intend to look out for something to laugh about today. Will you join me?

SUNDAY—FEBRUARY 11.

FOR we know that if our earthly house of this tabernacle were dissolved, we have a building of God, an house not made with hands, eternal in the heavens.   Corinthians II 5:1

MONDAY—FEBRUARY 12.

I RECENTLY came across this story of an elderly lady who had withstood the London blitz with amazing fortitude. She was a prime example of those proud Britons who were determined not to let the enemy's threats and actions win the day.

When asked the secret of her inner strength, she replied, "Well, every night I say my prayers and then I remember how the parson told us God is always watching, so I go to sleep. After all, there's no need for two of us to lie awake."

I WAS returning some books to the library the other day when I noticed on the young girl librarian's desk a "Thought for the Day" calendar.

"Do you ever take notice of the sayings?" I enquired.

"Oh, always, Mr Gay," was the instant reply. "Take yesterday, for instance. I had had a really awful morning. I arrived at work late, then at elevenses, I spilled a mug of coffee down my dress. Later, I missed the bus home at lunchtime. In the afternoon I discovered I'd been stamping all the books with the wrong date. It wasn't until later on that I realised I hadn't looked at the saying for the day. You'll never guess what it was."

She placed it in front of me and I read, "If there were no clouds, we should not enjoy the sun".

"It made me smile," she said, "and after that, everything went all right. I wonder why!"

I think we both knew.

WEDNESDAY—FEBRUARY 14.

MUCH has been written about the skill, the originality and business acumen of the famous potter, Josiah Wedgwood, but I came across a sidelight on this great man in an unexpected place — the writings of John Wesley.

After a visit to Burslem in 1760, Wesley said, "I met a young man by the name of J. Wedgwood who had planted a flower garden adjacent to his pottery. He also had his men wash their hands and faces and change their clothes after working in the clay. He is small and lame, but his soul is near to God."

What a lot those few lines tell us about a great and good man!

THE FRIENDSHIP BOOK

HERE is some sound advice from J. M.
Robertson of Edinburgh:

> Rub shoulders with Contentment,
> Make Happiness a friend.
> Run with Resolution
> Round each uncertain bend.
> Mingle with the Optimists,
> Whose fervour is for keeps,
> And remember that a man is known
> By the company he keeps.

WHEN the Lady of the House and I were on
holiday, we decided to spend a night at a small
private house offering bed and breakfast. The
bedroom was simply but attractively furnished and on
the wall hung a painting of the Good Shepherd.

As we settled down for the night, the Lady of the
House remarked that she didn't expect to sleep too
well as it was an unfamiliar bed, but the next morning
she said that, to her surprise, she had slept soundly.

Over breakfast we asked our hostess about the
picture. "Yes," she said, "it's a favourite of mine. It
belonged to my mother and that was her bedroom. All
her life she loved going to church and when she
became too frail to attend, she missed it terribly. So
every night before she went to sleep, I used to read her
one of her favourite Bible passages while she gazed at
the picture."

"Of course, Francis," remarked the Lady of the
House, smiling, "that explains why I slept so
peacefully last night. How could I fail to in a room
steeped in so many lovely thoughts?"

Who was I to disagree with that?

C

THE FRIENDSHIP BOOK

SOMETIMES there is so much dismal news that if we are not careful it can overwhelm us and make us dismal, too! It reminds me of a story from Ireland about a nightingale.

One day, a shepherd called to a nightingale, "Please sing, lovely creature!" However, the bird would not sing, and replied, "What's the use? The frogs are making too much noise. It takes all the pleasure out of singing. Can't you hear them?"

The shepherd replied, "Of course, but it's only your silence that allows me to hear them."

The nightingale was silent for just a few moments longer. He hated the dismal croaking of the frogs, but he loved the shepherd and so sang out in a beautiful, clear voice.

"Thank you," called the shepherd. "Your cheerfulness has brightened my day. Never let the dismal ones have all the say again!"

SUNDAY—FEBRUARY 18.

HEAVEN and earth shall pass away: but my words shall not pass away.   Luke 21:33

MONDAY—FEBRUARY 19.

I THINK the word "kindness" is one of the most beautiful in the English language. It is also one of the most important. Without kindness, life would be dreary indeed.

> *Kind hearts are the gardens,*
> *Kind thoughts are the roots,*
> *Kind words are the blossoms,*
> *Kind deeds are the fruits.*

THE FRIENDSHIP BOOK

ONE of the nice things I have heard about recently was a project by Dr John Hull of Birmingham University called "Touch and Hearing" which was started to help blind people to enjoy the beautiful cathedrals they are unable to see.

The idea was born when Dr Hull lost his own sight. When he visited a cathedral with his wife, he realised that although *he* retained some visual memory and could understand the taped commentaries, people blind from birth would be unable to comprehend the beauty of sunshine filtering through a stained glass window.

However, listening to the organ, a magic sound even for the sighted, was like turning on the lights for a blind person. Similarly, as Dr Hull was encouraged by his wife to hold on to one of the great cathedral pillars, feel his way around it and touch the carving, he could imagine the size of a cathedral which needed such a massive column to support it.

In many other ways, Dr Hull found it was possible to make the sights, sounds and dimensions of cathedrals come alive for the blind. How good it is when even our misfortunes can be used to assist others!

OUR friend Jessica was trying to teach her two-year-old son how to say "Please" and "Thank you". She gave him a biscuit and asked, "What do you say?"

"Please," replied Mark.

"No, what do you say after you've been given something?"

"More please," came the reply.

THURSDAY—FEBRUARY 22.

CHARLES EAMER KEMPE was a Victorian craftsman who filled the windows of many of our cathedrals and parish churches with stained glass of exceptional quality. His Pre-Raphaelite figures with their noble faces and subdued colours are quite exquisite.

Kempe had initially wished to enter the Church, but a speech defect made him decide instead to develop his talent for working with stained glass in order to enhance the House of God. It is said that when he was a child, he had a mystical experience in Gloucester Cathedral, induced by the setting sun casting its rays through the cathedral's windows, and significantly his first window was made for that cathedral.

He believed that man's highest endeavour should be to glorify God, and he used his wonderful skills to that end.

FRIDAY—FEBRUARY 23.

THE other day I visited my friend Terry who is confined to the house with lumbago. He winced visibly as he moved across to greet me, and involuntarily I winced with him!

"Is it bad today?" I asked.

"It is at the moment," he replied, "but it will go." He paused, and then added, "You know, that's one thing about pain, Francis — generally, it *does* go away. It seems to fill our lives while it persists, but when it's gone, we very quickly forget it. Think of all the aches and pains we suffer in life — toothache, headaches, cuts and bruises. As soon as they've gone, we never give them a thought, do we? Anyway, that's my philosophy!"

And a very good one, too.

OOD OLD WAYS

*D*ON'T be always putting off
    The things you mean to do,
Answering that letter,
Picking up the phone,
Speaking to an absent friend
Who's feeling all alone.

Tackle one job every day,
That's waiting to be done—
A job that you've been
putting off,
A job that could be — fun!

Anne Kreer.

NOW the God of patience and consolation grant you to be likeminded one toward another according to Christ Jesus.   Romans 15:5

A FRIEND of ours in the USA lives with her widowed father — a charming old man really, but he sometimes likes to put on an act of being a bit crusty.

She took him shopping recently in a big store and seeing he was looking a bit tired she said, "Let's take the elevator."

"Elevator!" he retorted, "why do you use these high falutin' words, Eleanor? It's a lift! You can lift people up and you can lift them down, but you can't elevate them down!"

He has a point there, hasn't he?

TUESDAY—FEBRUARY 27.

ONE morning, not long after the end of the last war, Charlie Brookfield seemed to have got out of bed on the wrong side. He'd expected bacon and eggs, and complained when he was given a kipper instead. The news in the morning paper didn't suit him, either, and the children were making too much noise. It really wasn't Charlie's day, and he was letting everyone know it.

Quietly, his wife moved across to a drawer in the bureau and took out a large envelope. "Charlie," she said, "I was looking at some of the letters you wrote to me when you were in the Forces. Do you remember this one, dated February 1945? Listen: 'Food awful, conditions terrible. If I ever get home I'll never complain about anything again!'"

You'll not be surprised to hear that Charlie didn't say another word. Instead, he just gave her a great hug and the biggest kiss he'd given her for a long time.

WEDNESDAY—FEBRUARY 28.

A FRIEND sent me this item from his church magazine, but I think you will agree that it applies to much more than the life of the Church:

"There were once four people — Everybody, Somebody, Anybody and Nobody. There was an important job to be done and Everybody was asked to do it. Everybody was sure that Somebody would do it. Anybody could have done it, but in the end Nobody did it. Somebody got very angry over this because it was really Everybody's job. Everybody thought Anybody would do it, but Nobody realised that Everybody wouldn't do it. It ended up that Everybody blamed Somebody when actually Nobody had asked Anybody."

MARCH

THURSDAY—MARCH 1.

I MUST confess that I am not very fond of leeks though I daren't say so today, St David's Day, when many Welsh people will be wearing one. Some though, will sport a daffodil instead, arguing that it is the true Welsh emblem.

Whichever side of the argument you take, there are certainly many legends connecting the leek with St David, the 6th century abbot-bishop who became the patron saint of Wales. He was a good man who led a simple, ascetic life, and contemporary accounts tell of him existing on a diet of leeks gathered from the fields and water from mountain springs.

In this world of plenty in which so many go hungry, I will be thinking today of this long-ago saintly man who followed the dictum "to live more simply that others may simply live".

FRIDAY—MARCH 2.

THE Lady of the House is on the rota of helpers at a local retirement club. The secretary collects newspaper cuttings, verses, cartoons and quotations and each week she puts one up on the notice-board for all to read.

The other day the Lady of the House showed me the previous week's cutting.

It said: "Old Age, believe me, is a good and pleasant time. It is true that you are gently shouldered off the stage, but then you are given such a comfortable front stall as a spectator, and, if you have really played your part, you are more than content to sit and watch." (Jane Ellen Harrison 1850-1928).

THE FRIENDSHIP BOOK

THE stars like jewels shine at night,
The Alps are crowned with snow,
How wonderful a Springtime wood,
A field where daisies grow.
But, to the housewife, bless her heart,
There's nothing quite so fine
As sun-warmed, wind-blown washing that's
A-drying on the line.

LET brotherly love continue. Be not forgetful to entertain strangers: for thereby some have entertained angels unawares. Hebrews 13:1-2

IN the hills of the West Riding of Yorkshire is a village called Shelf whose name is believed to have come from an old inn there.

In the days when wool was spun and woven in moorland cottages, the heavy pieces of cloth had to be taken by packhorse into the valley to be sold. Outside the inn at Shelf was a long passage with just room for the horses to stand, and there was a shelf at either side so that the heavy packs could rest there to ease the animals' backs without the bother of unloading. When the packmen and animals had rested, they were able to continue with their journey.

I often think that these platforms are like our "shelves of friendship", the unexpected phone call or letter, the invitation to a cup of tea or outing, or welcome knock at the door. They're all things that do so much to ease our load and help us on our way — and that we can do to help others.

TUESDAY—MARCH 6.

IT'S Springtime — and, as the Bible writer reminds us, "The time of the singing of birds is come."

I never cease to marvel at how they migrate thousands of miles in the Autumn and return in the Spring.

In the 13th century, a Cistercian monk conducted one of the earliest experiments in bird-ringing to find out their movements.

Noticing that the same swallows seemed to return to the eaves above his cell year after year he captured a bird and fastened a small piece of parchment to its leg. On this, he had written in Latin, "O swallow, where do you live in the Winter?"

The following Spring the bird returned with a message similarly written, but in Greek, "At the house of Petrarch in Antioch."

It has been happening for centuries, this quiet, regular, dependable miracle of migration — one of the many reminders, amid so much stress and strain and unrest in the world, that, "while the earth remaineth, seedtime and harvest, and cold and heat, and Summer and Winter, and day and night shall not cease."

WEDNESDAY—MARCH 7.

A FRIEND of ours who works for a large company has just changed his office. He's still in the same building, but in a different part. I liked his assessment of his new surroundings: "We are now on the north side where we don't get so much sun — but the view is far more pleasant."

We sometimes say, "You can't have everything," and that is all too true; but how much better it is when we can appreciate what we have gained instead of deploring what is lost.

THURSDAY—MARCH 8.

WHEN Derek lost his wife recently after a long illness, he found great comfort in these beautiful words written by Canon Henry Scott Holland, the much-loved Anglican philosopher and theologian:

"Death is nothing at all. I have only slipped away into the next room. I am I, and you are you; whatever we were to each other, we are still. Call me by my old familiar name, speak to me in the easy way we used to. Put no difference in your tone, wear no forced air of solemnity or sorrow.

"Laugh as we always laughed, play, smile, think of me, pray for me. Let my name be ever spoken without effort, without trace of shadow. What is death but a negligible accident? Why should I be out of mind because I am out of sight? I am but waiting for you, for an interval, somewhere very near, just around the corner. All is well."

FRIDAY—MARCH 9.

I'M sure all of us who have been inspired by the magic of Yehudi Menuhin's violin must have been happy when the Queen made him a member of the most exclusive circle in the world — the Order of Merit.

Menuhin was very moved by the award and what he said demonstrated the modesty of this brilliant man: "I'll have to practise harder to keep up my standard. I want to show I haven't received the award for things I've done in the past, but for things I'll do in the future."

Maybe that sounds just a little mixed up, but what an example his life is to any of us tempted to say: "That's not bad. It will do."

SATURDAY—MARCH 10.

I HAVE heard some eloquent preachers in my time and some of them used magnificent and impressive language. I doubt if any of them, however, could match the simple sincerity of this little prayer sent to me by D. J. Morris. I have treasured it ever since:

> *Thank you, God, for my daily bread,*
> *Thank you, God, for the books I've read,*
> *Thank you, God, for the prayers I've said,*
> *Thank you, God, for the way you've led.*
> *Thank you, God.*

SUNDAY—MARCH 11.

AND Jesus looking upon them saith, With men it is impossible, but not with God: for with God all things are possible.   Mark 10:27

MONDAY—MARCH 12.

DURING the early stages of the building of Liverpool Cathedral, an American visitor approached a workman and asked him what he was doing. The man replied, "I'm mixing mortar."

The visitor asked a second man, "And what are you doing?" to which the workman replied abruptly, "Carrying bricks."

The American then went over to a third man, a bricklayer, and asked him the same question. The man drew himself up to his full height and answered proudly, "I am building a cathedral."

Perhaps our lives would be more fulfilled if we regarded our simple daily tasks in the same light as that of the third man.

THE FRIENDSHIP BOOK

HERE is a poem for Springtime sent me by Margaret H. Dixon of Reigate:

VIOLETS

They are not large, yet everywhere
To watchful, waking eyes,
They fill the heart with wonderment
And simple, sweet surprise.

Half-hidden 'neath a bushy shrub,
And almost out of sight,
This very gentle little flower
Fills Springtime with delight.

For, like love's little duties done,
When no-one else can see,
They have a fragrance all their own,
Precious to you and me.

And more to God, who measures not
The greatness of the task,
But that we shed love's tenderness
On others, as we pass.

THERE are times when we feel overwhelmed by the scale of the world's problems, and think that there is so little we can do that it will make no difference.

I like the thought of a Christian Aid speaker who was quoted as saying, "Try to think of the little you can do not as a mere drop in a bucket, but as a drop of oil in a very hot machine."

THE FRIENDSHIP BOOK

CHARLES SPURGEON was such a wonderful preacher he held a congregation of 24,000 spellbound in the Crystal Palace. But he believed actions were more important than words, and he made an appeal to his congregation to embark on some great new work and to provide the money for it.

His appeal was answered by Mrs Anne Hillyard, a clergyman's widow, who wrote offering £20,000 to found a home for orphan boys. Spurgeon immediately visited her and thanked her for her gift of £200.

"Did I write that?" she asked. "I meant £20,000."

"Oh, yes," said Spurgeon, "you did put £20,000, but I was not sure whether a nought or two had slipped in by mistake and I wanted to be on the safe side."

This happened in 1866 and soon 12 orphans were being cared for, the start of the wonderful organisation that came to be known as Spurgeon's Homes.

Regardless of race or creed, it has given a new start in life to thousands of youngsters who would otherwise have faced a bleak future.

YEARS ago I used to visit an old lady who was very fond of having motto cards hung about the house. One I remember said:

> The beauty of the home is order;
> The blessing of the home is contentment;
> The glory of the home is hospitality;
> The crown of the home is godliness.

I am sure that is as true today as it was all those years ago.

THE FRIENDSHIP BOOK

JOHN MURRAY, the publisher, was a man with a wry sense of humour. On one occasion he wrote this characteristic note to a budding author:

"Sir, I have your manuscript, and it is like a precious jewel. And like a precious jewel, it will sparkle the more if cut."

That's true of so many things in life, isn't it? Cut out the padding, and the result will be much more effective.

GO ye therefore, and teach all nations, baptising them in the name of the Father, and of the Son and of the Holy Ghost.   Matthew 28: 19

A KING had planted a beautiful garden and one day he walked round it to see how everything was growing. To his disappointment he found that all the things he had so lovingly nurtured were complaining.

"If only I were strong and sturdy like the oak tree," moaned the cedar. "Why can't I be upright like the cedar?" asked the vine. "If only I could bear luscious grapes like the vine," sighed the rose bush.

Eventually, the king came to a solitary daisy with its face opened to the sun.

"Well, little daisy, and are you unhappy, too?" he enquired.

"Oh, no," replied the daisy. "When you planted your garden I think you wanted me in it, just as I am, and so I'm going to be the best daisy I can be."

A silly story? I don't think so. For doesn't it say a lot about the blessing of contentment?

GOLDEN HARVEST

Throughout the frosty Winter
Nothing stirs — and yet,
Fulfilling every promise,
Spring does not forget,
As April sunshine's gentle glow
Welcomes the daffodils below.

C

THE FRIENDSHIP BOOK

L IFE is not meant only for living, but for loving, too.

Some of us will remember the popular television programme "Doctor Finlay's Casebook" about the two Scottish doctors Cameron and Finlay, in Tannochbrae with its grey stone houses and farming community.

I once heard the actor Andrew Cruickshank, who portrayed Doctor Cameron, talking about his life and career. I found that he was an outward-looking man with a great concern for other people. It requires self-discipline and firm conviction to be like this; every actor has to have a certain inward-looking aspect to life to best express his art.

Andrew was very firm about his relationships with others. "These go on from the moment we are born to the moment we die — so they should dominate our thinking," he said.

If love for others takes the place of selfishness, life is happier and more worthwhile. Love is indeed the power which transforms the world.

A N old lady who suffers from arthritis tells me that she likes going on holiday to a hotel which has a beautiful ballroom. She can no longer dance herself but she loves to watch others.

"It's such a lovely sight," she says, "and you'd be surprised how many of the couples stop to talk to me. They make me feel part of what is going on."

It's a lovely thought that we might make someone who feels a bit left out of things, suddenly feel very involved, and happy for being so — just by talking to them. Try it today!

D

THE FRIENDSHIP BOOK

AN elderly woman slipped and fell in a busy street. Passers-by hastened to assist her, but she was already struggling to hoist herself up.

"Thanks, I'm all right," she assured them. "I always fall forwards, never backwards."

Nevertheless, she accepted help to a seat in a nearby store. "I seem to be very fond of kissing my native town," she mused wryly.

Obviously she knew how to take life's tumbles with a smile, and the incident made me think. We can't all fall forwards physically when our feet stumble; sometimes we inevitably fall backwards.

But when life gives us a hard knock mentally, we *can* try to take it courageously so that we "fall forwards" — that is, looking to the future instead of dwelling on the past. In the words of Aldous Huxley: "Experience is not what happens to a man; it is what a man does with what happens to him."

THINK only thoughts of love today
With understanding as your guide.
For you can help along their way
The weary ones who cross your path,
And cheerfully greet the folk you meet
And spare a while to listen to
That lonely woman in the street,
That boring person on the phone.
Perhaps she needs a friendly smile,
That woman with the screaming child?
And surely you can stop a while
To help them both get off the bus.
In helping others in this way
You'll make this such a happy day.

Joyce Frances Carpenter.

THE FRIENDSHIP BOOK

I HAVE come across scores of "secrets of happiness" over the years, but I think that of our old friend, Mary, takes a lot of beating.

Once, when she had been going through a particularly trying period of illness, I asked her how she managed to remain so cheerful and she replied, "Well, it's quite simple, really, Francis. Every morning when I wake up I say to myself, 'I am going to be happy today'. And I just am!"

Well, it certainly works for Mary. How about trying it for yourself?

BEHOLD, I stand at the door, and knock: if any man hear my voice, and open the door, I will come in to him, and will sup with him, and he with me.   Revelations 3:20

A SUPPORTER is someone who is on your side, in good times and bad. Or so it should be, though some of us are not very good supporters, I suspect.

I'm thinking of something I heard the other night when I was visiting a boys' club and got talking to the manager of their football team. He said there were two kinds of greeting when we walked through the small town where he lived.

When the team was doing well, some people would say, "*Our* team's doing well these days, Bill."

After a few bad results, the greetings became, "*Your* team isn't doing all that well these days, Bill."

Let's promise ourselves we will never be what used to be known as "fair weather friends".

TUESDAY—MARCH 27.

I HAVE Alice Christianson of St Catherines, Ontario, Canada, to thank for this delightful poem:

One of the nicest times of day
I'm sure you will agree,
Is when you put the kettle on
At four o'clock for tea.

The little tray's arranged with care,
Especially for two,
With dainty, tasty sandwiches
And biscuits, just a few.

The bright, round teapot's waiting for
The kettle's cheerful tune,
And a friend has come to share with you
A happy afternoon.

WEDNESDAY—MARCH 28.

THE children at a local primary school have an annual leavers' service for those who have reached the ripe old age of eleven and are going on to secondary schools. Each child is presented with a Bible.

Last year the vicar spoke to them of this important step on their journey of life. He told them, "God often takes us by mountain paths to show us the source of his streams." And he went on, "Always try to remember that worry's feet are mostly wearied by climbing hills before they are reached."

He finished with this advice: "Try, on life's journey, not to be one of those so bent on watching your step, that they get no joy from the scenery."

GOLDEN REST

THE FRIENDSHIP BOOK

SOME electricians were installing new lighting in the roof of Liverpool Cathedral. One accidentally left the lift doors open, thus making it impossible for anyone to call it down again.

Visitors to the Cathedral, gazing in rapture at its many beauties, were somewhat startled to hear the Clerk of Works yelling heavenwards, "Peter, close the gates!"

A YOUNG woman kept praying and praying for the welfare of her son who was kicking over the traces. As time passed, he seemed to drift farther from her and she was on the verge of despair. However, her elderly Bishop urged her to continue praying. "It is impossible," he said, "that a son of so many prayers will come to a bad end."

And at last, Monica's prayers were answered. Her son changed. Augustine became a Christian, was baptised, and within eight years became a Bishop himself and a tower of strength for others.

AS a candle's cheerful light
Scatters all the gloom of night,
Hope will come a-shining through,
Lighting up the way for you,
Glowing through the darkest days,
Sending out its healing rays,
Beaming like a leading light,
Until once more the way is bright.

Dorothy M. Loughran.

APRIL

SUNDAY—APRIL 1.

Hold fast the form of sound words, which thou hast heard of me, in faith and love which is in Christ Jesus.   Timothy 1   1:13

MONDAY—APRIL 2.

THE names of all our months are of Roman origin. Some of them are called after Roman emperors — July (Julius) and August (Augustus). Others are from gods and goddesses — January (god of the doorway) and May (Maie, goddess of fertility).

I especially like the name April which comes from the Latin word *aperire,* "to open" — very apt when you think of how buds and blossoms unfold in the Spring.

The month of "opening" . . . The earth has been "shut up" during the Winter — hard and bare and many of us have been "shut in" too, unable to get about as much as we would like. Now, like the trees and shrubs, we, too, are unfolding, opening up to Springtime.

TUESDAY—APRIL 3.

TWO women who had met casually at a social gathering started talking about their respective families. One was surprised to find that not only did the other woman have seven children, but that the eldest, Mary, had been adopted a few years previously.

"Gracious!" she exclaimed in astonishment. "Didn't you have enough of your own?"

"Well, yes," replied the other quietly, "But Mary had no one at all."

THE FRIENDSHIP BOOK

ONE grey, wet day I dropped in on our old friend Mary and found her searching through her autograph album.

"Ah," she said suddenly, "this is what I've been looking for."

It was a verse by the American writer and preacher, the late Henry van Dyke:

If all the skies were sunshine,
Our faces would be fain
To feel once more upon them
The cooling splash of rain.

Somehow, after that, I didn't mind the prospect of a wet walk home.

HENRY MOORE, the sculptor, who died in 1986 at the age of 88, once said that he preferred to sit on a pebble beach rather than on golden sands. For him each pebble had its own texture, its own feel and individual shape. Some were more exciting than others, he said, but all were interesting and equally worthy of studying.

The great sculptor must have treated people in much the same way. When he died he was mourned not only as a talented artist, but as a man generous with his praise for the work of others less able than himself. Many remembered him as a man who was always busy, yet always found time to encourage others.

Few of us will ever, like him, change stones into works of art, but we can all be skilled in the art of living. Our friends and relatives are like Henry Moore's pebbles — all interesting in their own way and each one deserving attention.

FRIDAY—APRIL 6.

THESE few lines of advice are by the poet Phyllis Ellison:

> Don't judge a book by its cover,
> Or people at first glance,
> You must read the pages of a book,
> Give people a second chance.
> You've got to get to know them
> Like the characters in a book,
> So don't judge them by their covers,
> Take a longer, closer look.

SATURDAY—APRIL 7.

A HYMN especially associated with Palm Sunday is "All glory, laud and honour, to thee, Redeemer, King", and it is sung in many of our churches on that day.

There is a nice story about its origin. On Palm Sunday A.D. 821, a crowd had gathered in the ancient French city of Angers to see the annual procession of dignitaries headed by the king, pass through the streets.

Their route went by the cloisters where Theodulph, Bishop of Orleans, had been imprisoned and deprived of his bishopric for supposedly plotting. As the procession drew level with his cell it came to a halt, for a voice could be heard singing something that they had never heard before, "All glory, laud and honour!"

The king listened, deeply moved, and when he discovered that the singer was the imprisoned Theodulph, he ordered his immediate release, and restoration as Bishop. Further, he commanded that the lovely hymn should be sung every year during the Palm Sunday processions.

THE FRIENDSHIP BOOK

THEN said Jesus to them again, Peace unto you: as my Father hath sent me, even so send I you.

John 20,21.

MONDAY—APRIL 9.

AS the Spring sunshine warmed the air I decided to open up my beehives. This is one of the most important times in the beekeeper's calendar and I was anxious to see how the bees had survived the Winter. Would they be active, free from disease and ready to go?

Bees are not a domesticated insect and we have to be constantly vigilant, to stop them from swarming and leaving us. We plunder their hives of honey and leave them substitutes instead. If honey was the only gift we received from them, then we should be amply rewarded, yet there is more to them than that. The murmur of bees amongst the flowers on a Summer's day should remind us that, as they suck nectar, they give life to future flowers yet unformed. So as a beekeeper, I never cease to marvel at the perfect relationship between man and insect, part of the many wonderful life-enhancing harmonies in this world.

TUESDAY—APRIL 10.

I F nobody smiled and nobody cheered,
And nobody helped us along,
If each every minute looked after himself
And good things all went to the strong;
If nobody cared just a little for you
And nobody thought about me,
And each stood alone in the battle of life,
What a dreary old world it would be.

THE FRIENDSHIP BOOK

STEPPING aside to let a young man and his companion enter a city library, I once more marvelled at the skill of that companion. He had guided his young owner up the steps and through the swing door without hesitating. The master was blind and his friend was his guide dog.

We are so accustomed to seeing guide dogs with blind people that we sometimes forget other canine working companions who help the disabled.

The Hearing Dogs for the Deaf scheme started in America in 1975 and spread to Britain. Dozens of dogs have been trained to warn their deaf owners by touch when they hear an unaccustomed sound or sense danger. These wonderful animals help in other ways, too, bringing greater independence and confidence to their owners.

The dogs provide not only help, but love and companionship, too, adding a new dimension to their owners' lives.

OUR young neighbour called round the other day to show us her new pendant, and very pretty it was, too. It was enamelled with a pattern of flowers on one side and a bright mosaic on the other, so that if it twisted round it didn't reveal a rough, unattractive side.

It set me thinking. Most of us find it easy to present our best side when everything is going well, but when we have an "off day", even our nearest and dearest may get the rough side of our tongue.

How much nicer it would be for those around us if our worse side could get a little bit more like our best side — just like Dawn's pendant, in fact!

HOUSE OF FAITH

Thank God for all the ancient crafts,
The vision clear of yesterday
That raised our sturdy monuments
Where all may worship, praise and pray.
Those workers long since turned to dust
Have left their vision in our trust.

WHEN are the best days of our lives? When we're very young, growing up, or at some later stage in adult life?

At all times there are things we dislike and others we relish. One five-year-old girl was heard to say, "I don't like school, but I think I might change my mind when I leave it!"

Every stage of life and work brings its problems as well as its joys, but the secret is surely in the attitude we adopt. Of course we want to succeed in whatever we attempt, and if we work with a spirit of goodwill towards all with whom we come into contact, together with an ability to accept ourselves as we really are — well, we have a good chance of a happy and contented life.

SATURDAY—APRIL 14.

HAVE you heard the legend of the dogwood? At the time of the Crucifixion, the dogwood was just as tall as any of the forest trees. It was so strong and straight that it was chosen as timber for the Cross.

To be used for such a cruel purpose greatly distressed the tree, but Jesus sensed this and promised, "Never again shall the dogwood tree grow large enough to be used as a cross. Henceforth, it shall be slender, bent and twisted, and its blossoms shall be in the form of a cross, with two long and two short petals. In the centre of the outer edge of each petal there will be nail prints marked with rust and in the centre of the flower will be a crown of thorns. And all who see it will remember."

If you look closely at the blossom of the dogwood, you will see these marks.

AND when Jesus had cried with a loud voice, he said, Father, into thy hands I commend my spirit: and having said thus, he gave up the ghost.

Luke 23:46

THERE is a familiar passage in one of John Masefield's plays which is well worth recalling this Eastertide. It's part of a conversation after the Crucifixion between a Roman centurion, Longinus, and Procula, the wife of Pontius Pilate:

Procula: Do you think he is dead?

Longinus: No, lady, I don't.

Procula: Then where is he?

Longinus: Let loose in the world, lady, where neither Roman nor Jew can stop his truth.

That is the essence of our Easter faith.

DRUM CASTLE is one of a marvellous array of old castles which dot the countryside of Aberdeenshire, and until recently, its lairds could be traced back in an unbroken line for several centuries. They included many outstanding men, but what impressed a friend of mine who went round Drum recently was a door in a little room. Through it could come tenants who wished to see the laird privately, without anyone else knowing their business.

"You know, Francis," said my friend, "that seemed to me the highest kind of courtesy. Whatever kindness the great man was able to do for his visitors was doubled by the consideration he took to understand their feelings and spare them any embarrassment."

THE FRIENDSHIP BOOK

RECENTLY, I came across this touching thought which is especially appropriate for Easter and all that the festival symbolises:

What is lovely never dies,
But passes into other loveliness.

HAVE I ever really thanked you, Lord, for the fact that I can see
A clear blue sky, a bird in flight, a child upon my knee,
A sunset's glow at eventide, a cloud so full and white,
In never-ending gratitude — the wondrous gift of sight?

Have I ever really thanked you, Lord, for the fact that I can hear
A bird in song, my children laugh, a spoken word so dear,
A welcome knock upon my door, rain on my window pane?
It means that I am part of things and have so much to gain.

Have I ever really thanked you, Lord, for the fact that I can walk
A country lane, a city street, meet friends and stop to talk,
To climb upon a hillside and marvel at the view?
All these things are blessings, gifts sent down by you.

We walk along life's highway, and seldom stop to say
Thank you, Lord, for all these gifts so dear to us each day.

Maralyn I. Fawcett-Smith.

FRIDAY—APRIL 20.

A MINISTER friend has just been telling me about an international Christian conference which he attended recently. He says that the most moving moments for him were in the closing devotions when the delegates from many countries were invited to say together The Lord's Prayer, each in his or her own language.

Of course the timing was all at sixes and sevens due to the different lengths of words and phrases in the various languages, so they did not all finish the prayer at the same moment. That didn't matter, however. What did matter was the wonderful sense of togetherness the delegates felt when repeating this universal "family prayer".

To say and believe the words of "Our Father" draws us all more closely together, whatever our differences.

SATURDAY—APRIL 21.

A PERSIAN king asked one of his wise men for a maxim which could be applied either to joy or sorrow.

The sage wrote: "This, too, shall pass away."

Life is very hilly, with many ups and downs. When we come to a rough patch, it is worth remembering that "this, too, shall pass away."

The Psalms remind us that "Weeping may endure for a night, but joy cometh in the morning."

Then there is the Bible's frequent phrase: "And it came to pass . . ."

We might regret the passing of joyful experiences, but I'm sure most of us will be glad to remember, when having a difficult time of it, that "this, too, shall pass away."

UP TO MISCHIEF

Pussy cat, pussy cat,
What do you see?
A sparrow, perhaps, in the apple tree?
Pussy cat, pussy cat,
Leave it there.
Chase our feathered friends if you dare!

E

THE FRIENDSHIP BOOK

SUNDAY—APRIL 22.

AND the Word was made flesh, and dwelt among us, (and we beheld his glory, the glory as of the only begotten of the Father,) full of grace and truth.

John 1:14

MONDAY—APRIL 23.

AN elderly couple I once knew had an umbrella each and when they walked in the rain they kept well apart to avoid tangling. Then, one day, the husband left his on a bus. It was especially annoying because shortly after they got off, it began to rain and he had to share his wife's umbrella.

They huddled together beneath it as they walked home and soon they were talking and laughing together. The husband even put his arm around his wife. It was easier keeping together under one umbrella that way!

I often think of that umbrella. It reminds me that sharing can bring us so much closer to each other. Possessions all too often separate us.

TUESDAY—APRIL 24.

I LIKE this inspiring verse by the Edinburgh poet, J.M. Robertson:

A mile of smiles is better
Than a marathon of moans.
Chasing after laughter
Is more fun than trailing groans.
The race of Life is hectic,
But when all is said and run —
When Optimism takes the lead,
Contentment can be won.

THE FRIENDSHIP BOOK

"WHAT a wonderful place this is!" remarked Mrs Jones, whose holiday in South America was the fulfilment of plans made well over six months earlier. But it so nearly didn't happen!

She had gone to her doctor's, feeling unwell, and was startled to hear that she wouldn't live to enjoy South America. But Mrs Jones had replied with spirit, "I bought new dresses and shoes for this holiday, and I'm not going to waste them. What can you do about it?"

The doctor thought it just possible that a drastic course of treatment might delay the inevitable, and so week after week for over six months, she underwent chemotherapy. To the doctor's amazement, he found that Mrs Jones was completely cured.

Mind over matter, or simply old-fashioned courage? No wonder Mrs Jones had such a wonderful holiday!

THOSE of us who gratefully remember the spiritual guidance we received in our homes from earliest days will gladly echo the words of the anonymous writer of this verse, especially as Mothering Sunday approaches:

I have worshipped in churches and chapels,
  I have prayed in the busy street;
I have sought my God and have found Him
  Where the waves of the ocean beat.

I have knelt in the silent forest
  In the shade of some ancient tree;
But the dearest of all my altars
  Was built at my mother's knee.

QUIET CORNER

FRIDAY—APRIL 27.

A FRIEND occasionally sends me a copy of his church's order of service leaflet which is always headed by a meditation for the week. A recent one carried the words of a Gaelic blessing which I believe could be a great help to many of us in times of stress and uncertainty:

Deep peace of the running waves to you;
Deep peace of the quiet earth to you;
Deep peace of the silent hills to you;
Deep peace of the flowing air to you;
Deep peace of the shining stars to you;
Deep peace of the Son of Peace to you.

SATURDAY—APRIL 28.

IT is an interesting and curious fact of history that so many parsons have, in the past, been involved one way or another in the wool and textile trade. "True Men of the Cloth" they have been called!

There was the Rev. William Lee of Nottingham who, as far back as the time of Elizabeth, patented a stocking machine. Then, in the 18th century the Rev. Edmund Cartwright invented the first power loom. A little later, the Rev. Samuel Marsden, a Yorkshire chaplain to a penal settlement in Australia, brought back from that country the first bag of Australian wool.

However, the member of this company who intrigues me most is the 19th century American, Pastor Isaac Lamb, who invented a knitting machine. When he had completed it after a long struggle, he is reputed to have prayed, "Dear Lord, impart to it the dexterity of the hand." I like that combination of human skill and of humility.

SUNDAY—APRIL 29.

THEREFORE if any man be in Christ, he is a new creature: old things are passed away; behold, all things are become new.　　　　　Corinthians II 5:17

MONDAY—APRIL 30.

THE sound of the "Slaves Chorus" from the opera "Nabucco" floated across the Italian countryside. The peasants were singing it as a tribute to their neighbour Guiseppe Verdi who had died on 27th January 1901.

If anyone had asked them why they had chosen that particular chorus from his many compositions, they would have declared it was their favourite — it spoke to them of struggles for freedom in their own land and the bond they felt with the Israelites of old.

Yet that chorus and its opera were written by a man who had previously vowed never to write another note of music. After early successes, his first opera "Oberto" failed. His personal life was in ruins after the deaths of his wife and children.

He had finished with music, he decided — life was not worth living. Even when Morelli, the impresario of La Scala in Milan, gave him a poem based on an Old Testament story to read as an inspiration, Verdi merely tossed it aside. Then, days later, something made him look at it. The words based on the Israelites' struggles in Babylon gripped his attention. Inspiration came to him and he began to write "Nabucco".

It was a triumph as were many of his later works. Guiseppe Verdi became world-famous, yet none of the tributes at his death were more sincere than the singing of his famous chorus by his peasant neighbours. Despite attaining great fame, he could still communicate with ordinary people.

MAY

TUESDAY—MAY 1.

TODAY begins what has traditionally been called "The Merrie Month of May", and for hundreds of years the first of May was marked by maypole dancing, May Queens, fairs and all kinds of festivities. Many of these customs have died out, though some have survived, and others, such as morris dancing, have been revived in recent years.

But don't let us forget what it is all about. Our May Queens may well be the descendants of Flora, the Roman goddess of flowers, whose festival of Floralia was held in homage to the renewal of life and beauty after the coldness and barrenness of Winter. Our May festivals, too, were to herald the coming of Summer.

Whatever the weather happens to be like today, we can take heart from those familiar words of an anonymous 13th century poet, "Sumer is icumen in". How welcome it is, too!

WEDNESDAY—MAY 2.

IT'S only eight lines long, but this simple poem by Glenda Moore says so much. She calls it her "Evening Prayer":

> Thank you, Lord,
>   For giving me today,
> Each splendid hour,
> To do with what I may,
> Each cherished moment,
>   To use at my behest,
> And thank you, Lord,
>   For evening and my rest.

PERFECT HOLIDAY

When sagging spirits we'd restore,
What better place than a sun-washed shore?

THE FRIENDSHIP BOOK

THURSDAY—MAY 3.

SOME years ago, a researcher in America set out to try to discover what it is which enables people to live to a great age. He interviewed 2000 folk who had lived to be 90 or more and asked them a great many questions about their lifestyle, habits and outlook.

Did they have a happy childhood? Had their subsequent lives been hard or easy? Had they enjoyed their work? Did they drink or smoke? Did they take plenty of exercise? Were they indoor or outdoor types? Vegetarians or meat eaters? When he analysed all the answers to his questions, he found that though they varied greatly, the old folk all had one simple thing in common: they had all learned the art of being content.

FRIDAY—MAY 4.

IN his fascinating book "Akenfield", the account of life in an East Anglian village, Ronald Blythe lets the villagers tell their own story.

One of them, Fred Mitchell, a retired horseman, was 85 when he was interviewed and he could look back over a long life of considerable hardship. "There was nothing in my childhood, only work," he said. "I never had pleasure. One day a year I went to Felixstowe along with the chapel women and children, and that was my pleasure. But I haven't forgotten one thing — the singing. There was such a lot of singing in the villages then, and this was my pleasure, too. Boys sang in the fields, and at night we all met in the forge and sang. The chapels were full of singing. When the First War came it was singing, singing all the time. So I lie — I *have* had pleasure. I have had singing."

A simple but moving tribute to the power of music in lightening life's burdens.

THE FRIENDSHIP BOOK

SATURDAY—MAY 5.

IT'S a fact that your viewpoint depends on where you're standing. I was in a large supermarket last week when a little girl called Katie went missing. An announcement was made over the public address system, and within minutes, a very relieved mother was able to collect her daughter from the manager's office.

Katie seemed unperturbed by the whole affair, but she did have a few stern words for her parent. "It's no use getting upset, Mummy," she said. "If only you wouldn't keep wandering off, you wouldn't get lost!"

SUNDAY—MAY 6.

AND the angel of the Lord appeared unto him and said unto him, The Lord is with thee, thou mighty man of valour.   Judges 6:12

MONDAY—MAY 7.

AREN'T those people lucky who are able to find great pleasure in the simple things of life? As the song says, "The best things in life are free".

Children know this. They love sand, water and lying in the grass, or catching leaves as they fall from trees in Autumn.

The writer G.K. Chesterton put it wonderfully when he wrote, "I do not think there is anyone who takes such pleasure in things being themselves as I do. The startling wetness of water excites and intoxicates me, the fieriness of fire, the steeliness of steel, the unutterable muddiness of mud."

I feel sorry for millionaires. They miss out on the great wealth of ordinary things. After all, becoming and staying a millionaire must be such a time-consuming and boring occupation!

TUESDAY—MAY 8.

ARE you worried? Anxious lest something go wrong? Take comfort and assurance from these wise lines by Anne Kreet:

> It may never happen . . .
> How often have you tried
> To set tomorrow's pattern
> With today as guide?
>
> How often have you panicked,
> Dreading things to come,
> Worried, and regretted
> The things you may have done?
>
> Yet, it may never happen,
> So, why fret in vain,
> Why cloud tomorrow's sunshine
> With unpromised rain?

WEDNESDAY—MAY 9.

BRUNO WALTER, the musical conductor, tells a memorable story about the time when Kathleen Ferrier, the famous singer, was touring America.

As he himself was busy with musical engagements, he was not able to act as her host, but he offered her the use of his home in Los Angeles. When he returned, the Austrian couple who looked after his home and cared for Kathleen told him that on her free evenings she would call them to the music room, sit at the piano, and to their delight, give them a private concert.

What a kind and thoughtful lady she was! And how right William Gladstone was when he said, "Be happy with what you have and are, be generous with both, and you won't have to hunt for happiness".

BRIGHT SPRING

THURSDAY—MAY 10.

WHEN Louis Pasteur, the French scientist, lay ill after suffering a stroke, the government stopped work on a laboratory it was building for him. When Pasteur heard this, his condition began to deteriorate rapidly and his friends begged Napoleon III to give orders for the work to be restarted.

Their request was granted and they hastened to Pasteur to tell him the good news. Immediately, he took a turn for the better. Indeed he recovered and was able to continue with his work for years afterwards.

Hope, indeed, is a wonderful medicine.

FRIDAY—MAY 11.

VISITORS to beautiful Keswick in the Lake District often call at St John's Church. Frequently they seek out the simple monument that marks the grave of Sir Hugh Walpole who helped to put this area on the literary map with his "Herries Chronicle".

Sir Hugh owned Brackenburn, a house perched in the hills above lovely Derwentwater. When he lived there, he was a regular attender of St. John's.

He had a simple Christian faith. Here is how he once defined prayer:

"Prayer is not asking for anything; it is rather putting oneself into contact with a world as you may pick up a telephone and speak to Persia. A world waiting to be visited. Your spirit is longing to go there — but for the most part, we are too busy, too tired, too egotistic, to take the trouble. But the more we do the easier, the more natural it becomes.

"That's what prayer is — moving from one country to another."

THE FRIENDSHIP BOOK

TODAY I would like to share with you a poem sent to me by Miriam Eker which she calls "Recipe For Life":

> *A little human kindness,*
> *Some tolerance and trust,*
> *A wish to help another,*
> *A love of all things just!*
> *A certain sense of humour,*
> *A very open mind,*
> *That's a recipe for Life,*
> *That anyone can find!*

MY soul hath a desire and longing to enter into the courts of the Lord: my heart and my flesh rejoice in the living God. Psalms 84:2

"TO make bread you need dough."

That was the headline that caught my eye recently, but it wasn't on the cookery page of the magazine that the Lady of the House had just put down.

No, the "dough" referred to was the money needed to send to the world's poorest people to help them to help themselves; to provide wells, grain, agricultural equipment, and to train people to develop the land and grow the food they need.

So, in Christian Aid Week from May 14th-19th, please remember that nobody can make bread without dough. As Francis Bacon truly said, "Money is like muck, not good except it be spread".

TUESDAY—MAY 15.

I CAN'T help wondering whether the Austrian Johann Mendel would ever have become famous if he'd achieved higher marks in biology and so obtained the teaching diploma he'd hoped for.

As it was, he entered a monastery and there had time to begin his study of hybrids in the garden. He found that some characteristics of living things were "dominant" and others "recessive", so discovering the basic law of heredity which became known as Mendel's Law.

For many years, nobody listened to him, and it wasn't until after his death that the importance of his discovery came to light.

The quiet abbot is now regarded as one of the giants of modern science.

WEDNESDAY—MAY 16.

L AST week, the Lady of the House and I felt very privileged. We were allowed to witness Graham, who's four, being put to bed, permitted to kiss his teddy bear goodnight — and granted permission to hear him say his prayers. It was the prayer many children learn to say:

> Thank you for the world so sweet,
> Thank you for the food we eat,
> Thank you for the birds that sing,
> Thank you, God, for everything.

As we tiptoed out, I found myself wondering who wrote these words. I discovered they came from the pen of an almost unknown housewife called Edith Rutter Leatham born in 1870. I doubt if more than one in a million knows her name, yet she bequeathed to every child this perfect little prayer.

Next time you hear a child speak its simple lines, remember her with thanks.

E

THE FRIENDSHIP BOOK

MRS CLARK was scolding her husband for forgetting her birthday:

"Why can't a man think of his wife a few years after marriage as he did before? It's just too bad! You've forgotten my birthday *again*. Only a few years ago, you declared that the date was engraved on your heart and you never failed to give me a present. Why not today?"

"My dear, I didn't wish to remind you that you are a year older," came the disarming reply.

FLASHES of wit are often voiced by the least likely people. Take, for example, the tale of the old Yorkshire dalesman when confronted with impatient tourists.

A motorist stopped and shouted, "Is this the way to Helmsley? Come on man, speak up! Can I get through this way?"

The old farmworker pondered. He did not like being hectored in such a manner.

"I don't rightly know," he said slowly.

"You don't know much!" snapped the motorist.

The dalesman grinned. "Maybe not," he agreed, "but I'm not lost!"

Complaints are often turned into jokes, especially in Ireland. There is a story of how a new postman had to walk up a very long lane to deliver a letter to a farm.

"It's a long lane to your farm," he complained to the farmer one day.

"Aye, 'tis," was the reply, "but if it were any shorter it wouldn't reach."

Such witty remarks are far better than angry retorts. They take the heat out of the situation and turn ill temper into laughter.

F

SATURDAY—MAY 19.

AFTER hearing of a friend's experience with a kind neighbour, a West Sussex reader sent me this rhyme:

"How much do I owe you?"
John's oldest neighbour said
When John had trimmed his hedge for him
— He's getting on, is Ted.

"I couldn't put a price on it!"
Was John's surprise reply.
"What do you mean?" Ted gasped aloud,
"The limit's not the sky!"

"I mean," said John, "You cannot cost
Help given by a friend.
Such aid is free as long as they
Have willing hands to lend."

SUNDAY—MAY 20.

FOR what shall it profit a man, if he shall gain the whole world, and lose his own soul?   Mark 8: 36

MONDAY—MAY 21.

WHEN I read the sayings of some of the great Chinese sages of long ago, I am impressed with how up-to-date is much of what they said. Here, for example, are some words of Lao-tse, founder of the Chinese religion of Tao 2,500 years ago:

"He who knows others is clever, but he who knows himself is enlightened. He who overcomes others is strong, but he who overcomes himself is mightier still."

THE FRIENDSHIP BOOK

HANNAH MORE was a godly woman, best known for her part in the formation of the Religious Tract Society.

She used to have a great way of dealing with gossips. Whenever anyone told her an unkind story about a neighbour, she would say, "Come with me now, and we'll go and ask the person if this is true."

The gossip would be appalled at the idea. "I'd rather not — there might be some mistake after all."

But Hannah More would always insist on going to see the person who had been slandered — and taking the gossip with her. That put a stop to a lot of loose talk!

AFTER Coventry Cathedral had been destroyed by an air raid in November 1940, a local rector noticed the floor covered with hundreds of nails — the long kind popular in mediaeval times. He picked up a few, took them away, and welded them into a quadratic cross which has four limbs of equal length, as in the Coventry Diocesan coat of arms.

A few days later, he took it to his Bishop, the Right Reverend Mervyn C. Haigh. The Bishop immediately said, "I have a meeting here this afternoon, and I'll put the cross on the table — but don't say a word to anyone."

This was the origin of the famous "Cross of Nails" — the symbol both of faith triumphant through suffering, and also of the new Cathedral's ministry of international reconciliation. A reminder of the positive truth of Christ's teaching is provided by the words carved on the walls of the present sanctuary: "Father, forgive".

THE FRIENDSHIP BOOK

A TEACHER asked his class their ambitions and received a variety of answers. Almost all the children, however, said they wanted to be famous.

The teacher decided to use this to encourage the children to work harder.

"Have you heard of Admiral Nelson?" he asked.

"Yes," they chorused.

"Well," said the teacher, "he worked hard — very hard.

"And have you heard of Abraham Lincoln?" he enquired.

"Yes, sir," came the reply.

"He was a hard worker, too. And have you heard of Simon Atkins?"

They hadn't.

"Ah, well, there you are," said the teacher. "*He* was a lazy good-for-nothing!"

B ARBARA JEMISON of Bridlington sent me these thoughtful few lines:

> *Let us never forget . . .*
> *The value of time,*
> *The success of perseverance,*
> *The pleasure of working,*
> *The dignity of simplicity,*
> *The worth of character,*
> *The power of kindness,*
> *The influence of example,*
> *The obligation of duty,*
> *The wisdom of economy,*
> *The virtue of patience,*
> *The improvement of talent,*
> *The joy of originating.*

REE'S COMPANY

THE FRIENDSHIP BOOK

SOME friends had to move to a new town. After a long journey they arrived at their house, very tired, and wondering what to do first. Before long, however, there was a knock at the door and there stood their new neighbour holding a tray with a pot of tea and a plate of sandwiches.

"I thought you'd be ready for a bite," she said, and went off with a smile.

"You have no idea what a difference that made to my day," said Molly later. "I had been so miserable about having to leave all my old friends that I hadn't even considered I would find such a good new friend so quickly."

It's something, perhaps, that many of us could bear in mind when someone new moves into our neighbourhood.

BE not curious in unnecessary matters: for more things are shewed unto thee than men understand.
                                        Ecclesiasticus 3:23

RECENTLY, I had the privilege of looking through the personal notebook which a friend had inherited from an elderly aunt. Amongst the variety of prayers and quotations that she had collected, this one was heavily underlined:

"Pause before you speak and ask yourself, is it true? Is it kind? Is it necessary?"

It is brief and to the point and, oh, what a lot of trouble could be prevented if more of us decided to follow that advice!

H AZEL AITKEN suggests a good way of falling asleep:

> *When you lie upon your pillow*
> *Count your blessings 'stead of sheep;*
> *Then you'll find a warmth enfolds you,*
> *Comforted, you'll drift to sleep.*
> *Days of sunshine, kindly actions,*
> *Children's laughter — on them think,*
> *Then you'll seldom need to grumble*
> *"Oh, I never slept a wink!"*

WEDNESDAY—MAY 30.

I LIKE this observation made by the French writer, André Maurois:

"Growing old is no more than a bad habit which a busy man has no time to form."

THURSDAY—MAY 31.

I AM always filled with admiration and awe when I see great things that man is capable of doing in music, painting, literature, sport and other fields. But these achievements don't come without effort.

Recently, I was reading about Holman Hunt who painted the picture of Christ entitled "The Light of the World". For three years he spent every moonlight night painting in an orchard in Surrey. He was determined to get the best possible mixture of light and shade in the background and each night he was outside for hours, his only protection a little shelter built of hurdles and a sack of straw to keep his feet warm.

He must often have been weary and extremely cold, but his dedication resulted in a wonderful picture that has brought comfort and hope to countless people.

JUNE

FRIDAY—JUNE 1.

IT was a beautiful day, and as I approached my friend Bertha's cottage, I could see she was busy in her garden. After greeting me she showed me the bowl she had filled with rose buds and petals.

"I'm making a pot-pourri," she told me. "I have picked all the heavily scented petals, and when they're dry and crisp, I'll sprinkle them with a few drops of rose oil and a tablespoon of orris root to make the perfume last.

"People have been doing this since the 16th century," Bertha continued, "but, you know, in those days they did it to disguise the unpleasant odours around their homes. Thankfully we don't need to do that nowadays," she smiled. "My home-made pot-pourri gives me lots of pleasure and it fills the cottage with the perfume and memory of my roses all through the Winter. I can close my eyes in December, and imagine it's Summertime!"

SATURDAY—JUNE 2.

I LIKE this short anonymous prayer I read recently:

Lord, make old people tolerant,
Young folk sympathetic,
Great folk humble,
Busy folk patient,
Bad folk good,
And make me what I ought to be.

They're all things that, put into practice, help us to treat our families, friends and neighbours with greater consideration — and make life as a whole run more smoothly.

THE FRIENDSHIP BOOK

AND Mary said, My soul doth magnify the Lord, And my spirit hath rejoiced in God My Saviour.

Luke 1:46,47

THIS notice was nailed up in the kitchen of a church hall, but I hope the writer didn't expect the helpers to carry it out literally!

"Will ladies kindly empty the tea pots, rinse round and before leaving, please stand upside down on the sink."

I'VE been reading a splendid book — a selection of entries from the diaries of men and women from all walks of life, some household names, others never known outside their own little circle.

And do you know what impressed me most? Not important people writing about important events, but a host of little things.

Samuel Pepys telling how he quarrelled with his wife and made it up; a housewife of 300 years ago writing of her worries about her family; Queen Victoria confiding to her diary how dearly she loved Prince Albert and how she hoped to marry him; a country clergyman visiting a sick parishioner and describing the little gift he was taking; an elderly gentleman much afflicted by a boil that wouldn't let him sit down . . . The list is endless.

All going to show that though we may think we've become so much cleverer, people have remained much the same through the centuries. We all have the same hopes and fears no matter which era we live in.

THE FRIENDSHIP BOOK

<u>WEDNESDAY—JUNE 6.</u>

I HEARD recently of a physical education teacher who retired after more than 40 years' work in schools. At his retirement party he told his colleagues, "In my young days I dreamed of being a great athlete, cheered by thousands to a string of world-breaking victories. Then I woke up to the reality that I didn't have the legs or the lungs. It didn't matter — it gave me the chance to help those more naturally gifted, and it's been great fun."

Then to his pupils he said, "Be a tug if you can't be a liner, for then you may give someone else a start."

<u>THURSDAY—JUNE 7.</u>

GLADYS, in Wales, was a bit surprised when her parents wrote to her from their home in the USA asking what sort of memories she had of her childhood. They had been visited by a nephew who had been telling them about his own childhood which seemed to have had more bad times than good. Gladys's parents hoped that she didn't feel that way, too.

Well, Gladys thought back over nearly 40 years, and remembered scores of happy times they had shared as a family. She made some notes, intending to include a few reminiscences at a time in future letters.

Once she began to write, though, she couldn't stop! Each happy memory triggered off more and she ended up by writing one very long letter filled with happy recollections.

Her parents were so thrilled to receive it that they made a transatlantic telephone call to thank their daughter for one of the loveliest gifts they had ever received. After all, it had brought back wonderful memories to them, too!

THE FRIENDSHIP BOOK

FRIDAY—JUNE 8.

ST SAMPSON'S Old People's Centre in York is almost world-famous. As well as local people, visitors from all over Britain, Europe and America, Australia and New Zealand drop into this attractively converted ancient church.

What is more, they all seem to enjoy the "word tonics" compiled by the enthusiastic warden, Lewis Creed. Amongst his offerings for happiness is this one entitled "On Sharing":

If nobody smiled and nobody cheered,
And nobody helped us along,
If each every minute looked after himself,
And the good things all went to the strong.
If nobody cared just a little for you,
And nobody thought about me,
And we all stood alone in the battle of life,
What a dreary old place this would be!

SATURDAY—JUNE 9.

I LIKE this story which the singer Caruso used to tell against himself.

One Summer's day, he was driving through the country when his car broke down. He made for a nearby farmhouse and approached a man sitting on the porch step.

"Excuse me," he said, "I am Enrico Caruso, and my car has broken down. Could I please use your telephone?"

The farmer jumped to his feet and shook his hand. "I never thought I'd have anybody so famous in my little farmhouse!" he exclaimed, then called his wife.

"Ethel," he said, "I want to introduce you to the world-famous traveller, Robinson Caruso!"

THE FRIENDSHIP BOOK

SUNDAY—JUNE 10.

AND though I bestow all my goods to feed the poor, and though I give my body to be burned, and have not charity, it profiteth me nothing.

Corinthians I 13:3

MONDAY—JUNE 11.

I THINK my neighbour, George, must have one of the most beautiful gardens in the district. Passers-by often stop to admire it, and you can hear their compliments.

One Summer, I'd been having a bit of trouble with my roses and I decided to ask George's advice. As expected, he was very helpful.

"Thank you, George," I said, as I came away.

"Thank *you*, Francis," he said with great emphasis. I must have looked a little surprised because I couldn't see what I had done.

"I mean it," he said. "People often tell me how beautiful my garden is, but they don't often ask for my advice, and that's really the best compliment of all!"

TUESDAY—JUNE 12.

WE all make mistakes; we all do things we regret. Mrs D.J. Morris of Stockton-On-The-Forest, York, expresses what many of us must feel:

I didn't always choose the Way
That He had meant for me;
I didn't always do the thing
I should, as now I see;
Mistakes shine out like beacons
Now that time has done its test.
My only consolation?
I always did my best.

TIME TO SIT AND TALK

THE FRIENDSHIP BOOK

I WAS carrying an awkward parcel recently. The street was quite steep, I was a long way from home and I had just felt the first drops of rain.

Suddenly I saw a little boy coming my way. As he drew near I heard him singing softly to himself — perhaps a tune he had just been practising at school. As he saw me, he looked up and gave a smile of such complete happiness that I experienced what I can only describe as a sudden burst of delight.

I suppose it was nothing very much, really — just a smile from a happy little boy I happened to pass in the street. But I suddenly forgot all about the rain and my heavy parcel and reached home much more quickly and with a far lighter step.

HAVE you ever thought of writing a letter of sympathy to a bereaved friend — but then not done it? Perhaps you felt that nothing you could say would do any good, or that the sufferer wouldn't want to be bothered with letters.

How wrong that is! I know, because scores of people have told me so. When we have lost a lifetime partner or a dear friend, the world suddenly becomes a very lonely place, and at such a time the support of those around us is beyond price.

Many years ago the poet John Donne wrote: "No man is an island". But that is how we feel in bereavement — alone and isolated. Then the kind words of someone who is thinking of us in our sorrow is a comfort beyond price.

So, if you have thought about writing that letter of sympathy, don't put it off any longer. Sit down and write it!

THE FRIENDSHIP BOOK

"I JUST can't believe it," a friend of ours said. "It's the most wonderful surprise."

Out of the blue she had been promoted manageress of a branch of the retail business in which she has worked for many years.

It was quite unexpected because Wilma is, well, not so young. She thought job advancement had passed her by.

It proves the wisdom of what the 17th century Dr Thomas Fuller, clergyman and author wrote: "When our hopes break, let our patience hold".

The millionaire Henry Ford was right, too, when he commented, "Anyone who stops learning is old, whether it happens at 20 or 90. Anyone who keeps on learning not only remains young, but becomes constantly more *valuable* regardless of physical capacity".

THERE are many more prayers for mothers than fathers, so I was pleasantly surprised to come across this one:

> *Mender of toys, leader of boys,*
> *Changer of fuses, kisser of bruises,*
> *Bless him, dear Lord.*
>
> *Mover of couches, soother of ouches,*
> *Pounder of nails, teller of tales,*
> *Reward him, O Lord.*
>
> *Raker of leaves, cleaner of eaves,*
> *Dryer of dishes, fulfiller of wishes,*
> *Bless him, O Lord.*

THE FRIENDSHIP BOOK

I AM the living bread which came down from heaven: if any man eat of this bread, he shall live for ever: and the bread that I will give is my flesh, which I will give for the life of the world.   John 6:51

EVE WOODLEY of Romsey in Hampshire, tells me she often jots down poems and thoughts that occur to her. These are just four of the thoughts she has passed on:

If you are busy helping others, self is having a jolly good rest.

Even if I don't make my mark in the world, may I find my place.

One good deed should exceed another.

Nothing improves without persistence.

I HAVE a large lavender bush in my garden; the bees love it, and I enjoy watching them flying to and fro, gathering nectar. One day, a particularly industrious bee caught my eye — it was positively overloaded! Several times it tried to take off, only to topple back into the bush, and yet it still couldn't resist the call of the nectar! Up the stem to the flowerspike it climbed, time after time, trying to add yet more to its load.

Some of us are like that bee, aren't we? We overload our lives — we try to do too much within the limited hours of each day. And the result? Like that bee, we fall back again and again.

Remember this little story, when next you are tempted to try to cram too much into your life.

F

WEDNESDAY—JUNE 20.

" SMILE, darn you, smile", ran a popular song which older readers may remember. Margaret M. Dixon puts it more poetically:

It lights the face with beauty, entirely lifts the gloom,
As will a tiny lantern some corner of a room,
And the passer-by is gladdened, when someone stops awhile,
To have a little cheery word, made richer by a smile.

Smiling is so easy, and yet we often may
Neglect to light another's path in this quite simple way,
So, when the world is blanketed with mist and pouring rain,
Just smile — it could bring sunshine to someone's life again.

THURSDAY—JUNE 21.

THE dictionary defines a saint as a holy person and that's what most people think of when they look at mediaeval figures wearing a halo and portrayed in stained glass windows. But did you know that the New Testament definition of a saint is "any ordinary Christian believer"?

It's a comforting thought, isn't it? We don't need to spend our life in a monastery or convent. All we have to do is to carry out the job that has been given to us to the best of our ability and with a loving heart.

We may feel we have not much to offer, but we can all be a saint by caring for our family, befriending a lonely person, giving a helping hand or listening to another person's troubles.

Are you going to be a saint — today?

G

THE FRIENDSHIP BOOK

ARE you a worrier? We all are from time to time. I like this verse from Mrs D.J. Morris of Stockton-on-the-Forest, York, which tells one way of overcoming it:

I have worried and sorrowed and trembled
Lest troubles would come by the score,
I have swithered and fumed and I've fretted
But I don't do that any more;
I make up my mind that I'll face it,
I'll deal with the problem today,
And I can't quite explain
But I find, in the main,
That the trouble just trickles away.

SATURDAY—JUNE 23.

MUCH has been written about friends and friendships, a sure indication of the way people value them. Here is a selection of observations on the subject by some eminent people:

"The only way to have a friend is to be one." (Ralph Waldo Emerson).

"A man, Sir, should keep his friendship in constant repair." (Letter to Lord Chesterfield from Dr Samuel Johnson).

"I have no talent for making new friends, but, oh, such a genius for fidelity to old ones." (George du Maurier).

"Old friends are best. King James used to call for his old shoes; they were easiest for his feet." (John Seldon, lawyer and bencher of the Inner Temple, 1584 - 1654).

So, here's to old friends — and new ones, too, of course!

SUNDAY—JUNE 24.

HEAVEN and earth shall pass away, but my words shall not pass away.   Matthew 24:35

MONDAY—JUNE 25.

I LEARNED a fascinating fact about plant lore recently. Most people know that the 24th June is Midsummer's Day, but you may not know that it is also St John The Baptist's Day.

I discovered that the shrub associated with this day is the hypericum, and that the red spots on its leaves are said to have appeared when Herod sentenced John the Baptist to death. That's why it's popularly known as St John's Wort.

In olden times when people were very superstitious, it was the custom to hang flowers around cottages on Midsummer's Day to protect the occupants from danger, and St John's Wort was the favourite for the purpose.

TUESDAY—JUNE 26.

THE Lady of the House had spent all morning in the garden and when she came in to prepare lunch she was smiling.

"What a lot of happy memories there are in the garden, Francis!" she said. "There's the rose bush that dear Mrs Powell bought me because it has my name, the cherry tree we planted to mark our wedding anniversary, the forget-me-nots I brought back from holiday, and so many plants in the border that different people have passed on to me. I think of all our friends when I'm out there.

"And that reminds me," she continued thoughtfully. "I really must write to Rose . . !"

COMPANIONS

You're trying to say you love me?
Well, I adore you, too,
And the best thing about weekends
Is sharing them with you.
Aren't we lucky, for no matter the weather
Whatever we do, we do it together?

THE FRIENDSHIP BOOK

JEAN DERWENT is retired now after many years as a primary schoolteacher. Of the many amusing stories she has to tell, I like this one:

"A boy called Sandy had the irritating habit of leaving the classroom door open whenever he returned to the room. One day I lost my patience and said in the loudest voice I could muster, 'And who was born in a barn then?'

"Sandy's reply was instantaneous: 'Jesus, Miss,' he said innocently."

"THE secret of success is the capacity to survive failure," said Noel Coward.

No one can be successful all through life. We all must fail at times. Sometimes it is the result of circumstances we cannot avoid. And, of course, disappointment can be difficult to live with. It's too easy to think that everyone is talking about our failure.

In fact, often nobody but ourselves, our immediate family or close friends know we've failed an examination; failed to land that job; failed to acquire a substantial bank balance in spite of years of hard work and thrift. Or even failed to keep our temper when provoked!

Failure is not a disgrace — unless we dwell on it and let it sour our life. Instead we should study it; try to analyse what caused it. There must be lessons to be learned from it which will help in the future. For it's the future that matters.

As the novelist Howard Spring wrote in his autobiography, "It would be a poor life if we never played a game without the certainty of success; never waged a fight unless we knew we should win it".

THE FRIENDSHIP BOOK

I CALLED to see my friend Mary one Winter afternoon and found her settled cosily by the fire sifting through a trunk of old family treasures.

"I left this out for you to see," she said, passing me an opened autograph album with a verse carefully written in copperplate. This is what I read:

> *If all our life were one broad glare*
> *Of sunlight, clear, unclouded,*
> *If all our paths were smooth and fair,*
> *By no soft gloom enshrouded,*
> *If all life's flowers were fully-blown*
> *Without the sweets unfolding,*
> *And happiness were rudely thrown*
> *On hands too weak for holding —*
> *Should we not miss the twilight hours,*
> *The gentle haze and sadness?*
> *Should we not long for storms and showers*
> *To break the constant gladness?*

ARNOLD BENNETT'S novels with their background of the Five Towns of the Staffordshire Potteries made him famous. He was born in one of the towns and knew how grim life could be for the folk who lived in their mean streets. He knew what it was like to struggle, too, for he worked his way up from a job as a local journalist to become a world-famous author.

He was speaking from experience when he wrote, "The best cure for worry, depression, melancholy and brooding is to go deliberately forth and try to lift with one's sympathy the gloom of someone else."

Wise words, indeed.

JULY

SUNDAY—JULY 1.

BLESSED is the man unto whom the Lord imputeth no sin, and in whose spirit there is no guile.

Psalms 32:2

MONDAY—JULY 2.

THIS verse by Phyllis Ellison is not about a big world-shattering event, but it warms my heart and I hope it does the same for you:

I wondered, should I speak to her,
She was sitting all alone,
At a table that was close to mine,
Where I sat on my own;
"Well," I ventured with a smile,
"Isn't it fine weather?"
And before our coffees had gone cold,
Two strangers sat together.

TUESDAY—JULY 3.

ONE Summer day in the middle of last century, a girl called Cecil Frances Humphreys sat on the top of Grabhurst Hill, above the town of Dunster, not far from the coast of Somerset. She saw the ancient castle, built in 1070 and still occupied, the pack-horse bridge, quaint and beautiful, the old mill and the Priory Church. And beyond them, the glorious countryside.

Then she went home and wrote that hymn which we have no doubt sung many times: "All things bright and beautiful, all creatures great and small, all things wise and wonderful — the Lord God made them all."

We perhaps know her better by her married name — Cecil Frances Alexander.

A HANDSOME prince once went to see three beautiful sisters in order to choose one for his bride. He took with him three gifts wrapped in separate boxes, each tied neatly with satin ribbon. He presented these to the girls in turn and watched their reactions.

The first demanded scissors and quickly snipped the string to unwrap her present. The second called for a knife and immediately cut through the ribbon and tore open the parcel. The third sat down, and, slowly and carefully, loosened the knot and unfolded the paper. It took much longer, of course, but she was in no hurry and was delighted with her gift when it was revealed.

When the time came for the prince to choose his bride, he selected the third young lady because, he said, she had shown the quality he admired most — patience. He knew it would stand them in good stead in their future years of happiness together.

R UTH GRAHAM, the wife of the American evangelist, Dr Billy Graham, was often left alone at home when her husband was travelling round the world on his campaigns. She has told how great a part reading played at those times in counteracting her loneliness.

She says that often she had four books "on the go" at the same time — ". . . one book to stimulate me, one to relax me, one for information, and one for conversation."

She had surely discovered, as we all can, the truth of what Martin Farquhar Tupper, a 19th century writer said: "A good book is the best of friends."

THE FRIENDSHIP BOOK

I LIKE the story of an English girl in Bombay, who wandered through the bazaar one day and was fascinated by a couple of rather attractive woollen jumpers hanging up.

She asked the Indian standing outside the shop if she could try them on. "Of course, madam," he replied.

After she had done so, she said, "I'll take them both."

The Indian's face fell. "I'm sorry, but that will not be possible. You see — we are a laundry!"

EVERY July, in the West German town of Dinkelsbuhl, there is an annual children's festival called the Kinderzeche, which dates back over 350 years to the Thirty Years War.

Dinkelsbuhl was besieged by invading armies from Bavaria, and no one knew what was going to happen. After several weeks, most towns would have sent messengers to plead for mercy — but not the civic leaders of Dinkelsbuhl. The besiegers watched in surprise as a small boy emerged from the city gates with a branch of cherry blossom.

He was followed in turn by all the children of Dinkelsbuhl, walking in solemn procession towards the enemy camp. Every child carried a branch of cherry blossom to lay as the city's offering before the commander of the invading forces.

He was so surprised that he ordered his troops not to harm the town or its people in any way. This courageous act by the youngsters is commemorated to this day by the annual children's festival — "The Feast of the Cherries".

H

THE FRIENDSHIP BOOK

FROM that time Jesus began to preach, and to say,
Repent: for the kingdom of heaven is at hand.

Matthew 4:17

VISITING a friend in hospital I found him in a
cheerfully decorated, brightly-lit new ward.

"It must make you feel better just to be in a place
like this, Colin," I said approvingly.

"Yes, it works a bit like a tonic," he smiled. "And
yet you know, Francis, it's quite a relief when 'Lights
Out' comes at night and it's dark. I can really rest
then."

I understand how he felt. How grateful we ought
to be for what someone has called "the alternating
mercies of life" — day and night, silence and song,
light and darkness, rest and activity. Each brings its
own special blessing.

YOUNG Peter had started to learn the violin and
he and his family had gone through all the
excruciating sounds of a beginner.

At long last he was considered proficient enough to
be invited to join the junior orchestra. After his first
rehearsal, he came home, his eyes shining with
enthusiasm. "Mum," he said, "When I play with *them*
I sound good!"

And isn't this true of so many other things? To
share with friends in a task to be done, a burden to be
carried or a time of great happiness, can make all the
difference in the world.

THE FRIENDSHIP BOOK

ST. WILLIAM'S COLLEGE in York is a fine half-timbered building near the Minster. Thousands of tourists visit it each year, but not many know the story behind the man whose name it bears.

William was Archbishop of York in the 12th century. He was beloved by many, especially the poor and ordinary folk, but like many good men, he had bitter enemies. Always he prayed that their jealousy would be forgiven.

He died suddenly after taking Holy Communion and it was believed that a rival, an Archdeacon, had poisoned the wine, but nothing was ever proved. William died forgiving all his enemies for his was too great a nature to bear malice.

Something similar could be said about the great American President Abraham Lincoln. Emerson, the essayist, said of him, "His heart was as great as the world, but there was no room in it to hold the memory of a wrong."

The world today would be a different place if there were more like St. William and Lincoln.

TODAY, I'd like to share Fiona Germaine's poem "Vice-Versa" with you:

It's good to get a letter,
A greeting on the phone,
A parcel is a nice surprise
When you are on your own.

It's good to write a letter,
Call someone on the phone,
To send a parcel's a great idea
For it proves you're not alone.

FRIDAY—JULY 13.

HAVE you ever felt disheartened by a criticism of your actions which you felt was unfair? It's as well, at a time like that, to remember the advice of the philosopher Plato:

"When men speak ill of thee — live so that nobody will believe them".

SATURDAY—JULY 14.

JULY 15th is St Swithin's Day and I expect most of us are familiar with the rhyme:

St Swithin's Day, if it does rain,
For forty days it will remain;
St Swithin's Day, if it is fair,
For forty days it will rain nae mair.

Swithin lived in the 9th century, was known for his piety and eventually became Bishop of Winchester. After his death, he was buried in a simple grave in the churchyard, according to his wishes. A hundred years later, however, people wanted to honour him with a more elaborate tomb and so his remains were moved.

Soon afterwards, the rain began to fall heavily and they thought that it was St Swithin's tears of sorrow. So once again he was moved, this time to a place inside Winchester Cathedral. The sun at once began to shine, and the people believed that St Swithin was happy once more.

Since that time many have said that July 15th predicts the weather for the next 40 days and have watched it anxiously. But it is also said that if rain does fall on St Swithin's Day, then the apples watered by it are the juiciest you can get!

THE FUN OF THE FAIR

SUNDAY—JULY 15.

BLESSED is the man that hath not walked in the counsel of the ungodly, nor stood in the way of sinners, and hath not sat in the seat of the scornful.

Psalms 1:1˙

MONDAY—JULY 16.

*K*NOCK *at the door, face with a grin*
Neighbour who asks, "May I come in?"
Makes such a difference in a long day,
Just a wee chat, then up and away
Living alone, two flights of stairs
— Nice to have proof somebody cares.

TUESDAY—JULY 17.

I WAS interested to learn recently how J. Arthur Rank started his career in the film industry.

He was a dedicated Sunday School teacher and chairman of the British Committee of the World Sunday School Association. One day he remarked to a colleague, "It's time we started using more modern methods for teaching the gospel in Sunday Schools. We are using the same techniques that our fathers and grandfathers did, and taking no notice of the fact that children are going to the cinema two or three times a week."

This thought prompted him to buy a number of projectors to lend to Sunday Schools, only to discover there were no suitable films to show. With customary enthusiasm and perseverance, he set about making a series of films for children based on Bible stories.

Thus it was his zeal for Sunday School work which led him to discover his latent talent and laid the foundations for a lifetime of successful film-making.

THE FRIENDSHIP BOOK

"THE ground's so hard that all my plants are curling up and dying," a gardener friend told me. "We've had no rain for weeks!"

Lying in bed that night, however, I heard the wind rising, and eventually the sound of drops against the window pane told me that the drought was over.

As I lay there, I knew that many gardeners would be sighing with relief, but I couldn't help thinking how small our problems are in this green land of ours, compared with unfortunate places such as Sudan or Ethiopia.

We don't know what real drought is, do we?

WE'VE all spoken at one time or another of someone sticking to a task like a limpet. But did you know that some real limpets have to adhere to the rocks harder than others?

I certainly didn't till one Summer morning when I was walking along a beach with a naturalist friend. The tide was far out and the rocks were thick with limpets.

"They all seem to look the same," my friend told me, "but if you examine them closely, you'll see that the shells of the limpets which get the biggest pounding from the sea are usually steeper than those in more sheltered places.

"You see, they have to suck harder to keep a stronger grip on the rock, and the muscles doing this have the effect of changing the shape of the shell."

Walking home, I thought that in one way or another, we are all a bit like limpets. The tougher things are, the harder we have to cling, and so our character is moulded — rather like the limpet's shell.

THE FRIENDSHIP BOOK

FRIDAY—JULY 20.

A VERY successful businessman had this motto framed above his desk:

There is no art in doing extraordinary things, but in doing ordinary things extra ordinarily well.

SATURDAY—JULY 21.

WHEN Thomas Edison, the famous inventor, was once asked to give advice to a boy just starting work, he said, "Don't look at the clock." Nowadays the advice would probably be, "Don't be a clock-watcher."

Edison was certainly not ruled by time, otherwise he would never have managed to invent so many of the things we now take for granted: e.g. the phonograph and the first central electric power plant. He eventually held over 1,300 patents.

In recent times many of the young men and women — middle-aged ones, too — who have started their own workshops and craft studios have discovered their success has been boosted by not watching the clock.

William Cobbett, the author of "Rural Rides" and a keen agriculturalist, tells of a man who lost his job by insisting on going for lunch on the stroke of the hour although he knew his boss needed his services a little bit longer. As he was leaving one day, his employer told him not to come back.

It is often said that if something needs doing, then ask the busiest person you know to tackle it. He or she will *make* time, will "go the extra mile".

That phrase originated because a Roman soldier could compel one of the inhabitants of an occupied country to carry his baggage for a mile, but no farther. To "go the extra mile" came to mean doing more than was requested — and doing it willingly.

THE FRIENDSHIP BOOK

FOR I will give you a mouth and wisdom, which all your adversaries shall not be able to gainsay nor resist.
Luke 21:15

HOW thoroughly I agree with these lines by Dorothy M. Loughran:

> *Song of birds and hum of bees,*
> *Fragrant blossom on the trees,*
> *Promise of a harvest fair,*
> *Apple, cherry, plum and pear*
> *Ripened by the Summer sun,*
> *Abundance there for everyone;*
> *Earth's countless gifts are everywhere,*
> *Enough and more for all to share.*

ALL around us, people are hungry for praise. The adage that if you can't say something nice, say nothing at all, is only partly true. It's always easy to be generous with a compliment. It's not hard to give — that costs nothing.

Somerset Maugham once said, "People ask you for criticism. What they want is praise." A chosen few get badges, medals and decorations, or even a listing in "Who's Who", but everyone at some time deserves a word of praise.

A compliment should never be left unsaid. There's an old French proverb, "To speak kindly does not harm the tongue, nor the heart of him to whom I speak."

Few of us will appear in the Honours List, but we're all given the opportunity to elevate the spirit!

THE FRIENDSHIP BOOK

I HEARD the other day of a wedding at which the congregation couldn't help smiling when the bride and 'groom knelt together at the altar. Some kind friend had previously taken the bridegroom's shoes, and in white paint he had written on the sole of his left shoe 'HELP' and on the sole of the right shoe 'ME'!

THERE was much excitement in the audience at the Academy of Music, New York. The orchestra was in place awaiting the Leader, the celebrated Johann Strauss the Second, composer of so many well-known waltzes and other lively pieces. This was to be his first appearance in New York.

Strauss gave no indication of nervousness as he stepped on to the platform and began to play, but suddenly there was a bump and a snapping noise. He had slipped, fallen and broken his favourite violin. Unhurt, though shaken, he scrambled to his feet, took another violin from a player and picked up the tune as if nothing unusual had occurred.

Such an incident would have unnerved a lesser man, but nothing ever seemed to come between Johann and his music. Illness and breakdowns caused long pauses in his career, but after each severe ailment he returned to the musical world. He persisted in his boyhood's musical ambition even when his famous father, Johann the First, had declared that one musician in a family was quite enough.

Johann was not only keen to become a musician — he was also determined that any music he composed would make his listeners feel happier.

How well he succeeded!

THE FRIENDSHIP BOOK

THIS little poem by Phyllis Ellison makes me smile — and also gives me something to think about:

> We exercise our bodies,
>   Like to keep ourselves in trim,
> Exercise our minds,
>   So our faculties won't dim.
> But how often do we exercise
>   That most important place,
> And relax those tiny muscles,
>   That spread a smile across our face?

"IT is amazing what you find when you start looking," remarked the organiser of a "Victorian Day" in her city.

All types of Victoriana had turned up — small items of furniture, Great-Grandmama's dresses and bonnets, Great-Uncle Simon's top hat and frock coat in which he had been married, not to mention the Victorian cradle and christening robes. Then there was beautiful needlework, lace and wonderfully bound and illustrated books.

Some of these objects had been stored away in trunks and boxes in spare rooms or attics for many years, and often they were just thought of as "junk", if remembered at all.

Come to think of it, life's a bit like that, isn't it? Some of the old-fashioned virtues — kindness, courtesy, helpfulness — often appear to have been stored away and forgotten about. Yet in the hustle of modern life, we need them more and more. It would be good to give them a proper airing again.

KING OF THE CASTLE

THE FRIENDSHIP BOOK

AND God made two great lights: the greater light to rule the day, and the lesser light to rule the night: he made the stars also.   Genesis 1:16

MONDAY—JULY 30.

ANCIENT Greece was famous for its wise men. The names of some of them have survived through the centuries — Aeschylus, Homer and Socrates among others. However, there were many, too, whose names have been forgotten, but whose sayings are still remembered.

One such anonymous sage, who lived in Athens, was asked when injustice would vanish from the earth. He replied, "When those who are not wronged feel as indignant as those who are."

Yes, we can learn much from the wise men of the past.

TUESDAY—JULY 31.

MY old friend Mary loves to collect verses, prayers and sayings that give her help or comfort, and then she copies them into a special book in her beautiful copper-plate handwriting.

Sometimes when we are sitting quietly together, she will bring it out and share one of her treasures with me. Here is one that she gave me recently:

Lord, watch the garden of my life; protect it from rust — the blight of envy, bitterness and strife; keep all my pathways fresh and bright, let fruit and fragrance be combined, blended with tact and love and grace, so, through each season, all may find my garden a delightful place.

AUGUST

WEDNESDAY—AUGUST 1.

HAVE you heard of the pessimist who, when asked how he was, replied, "Oh, I have my bad days and my worse days"?

It reminds me of the days of the week as set down by James Joyce in one of his books — "Moanday, Tearsday, Wailsday, Thumpsday, Frightday, Shatterday"!

Sadly there really are people who seem to think like that. How much happier they would be if they learned to say daily, in the words of the Psalmist in the Bible, "This is the day which the Lord has made. Let us rejoice and be glad in it."

THURSDAY—AUGUST 2.

THERE was a lovely copse close to a village I know. The villagers loved it, and there was great dismay when they heard it was to be cut down and the site used for a housing development. They got up a petition, held meetings and did all they could, but it was no use — the wood was felled and the houses built.

Perhaps not surprisingly many of the locals resented the newcomers who, unwittingly, came to live on the new estate. It wasn't until one weekend, at the annual church fête, that attitudes began to change. The newcomers brought in not only lots more people to swell the funds, but also new ideas, technical skills and, most importantly, new life into the annual event and the community as a whole.

The village may have lost a beauty spot, but it has gained a future.

FRIDAY—AUGUST 3.

HERE is a note from the end of a service paper from a church which the Lady of the House and I visited when we were on holiday:

"You might like to make a note of the hymns we have sung in our service this morning, then you can sing, hum or whistle them to yourselves during the coming week. It will remind you of our service and will help you to carry Sunday into your weekdays."

"Carrying Sunday into our weekdays" — now, there's a thought for us all to take to heart.

SATURDAY—AUGUST 4.

"THANK YOU" is one of the shortest phrases in the English language but the gratitude it expresses can often be profound. These anonymous lines put it neatly:

"Thank you" is something people say
For kindnesses that come their way,
Thoughtful things that others do,
Things that mean "I thought of you".

"Thank you" means that someone shared,
Someone loved and someone cared;
It means that someone had a part
In lightening someone else's heart.

George Herbert must have had similar thoughts many years ago when he wrote, "Thou who hast given so much to me, give one more thing — a grateful heart".

SUNDAY—AUGUST 5.

AND he said unto them, Why are ye so fearful? How is it that ye have no faith?   Mark 4:40

MONDAY—AUGUST 6.

IN his autobiography, Lord Mackintosh the toffee manufacturer tells a story of his younger days when a learned university professor had been invited to address the Mutual Improvement Society of his Chapel.

Mistaking the time of the meeting, the professor had arrived an hour early, and when Lord Mackintosh got to the hall he found the distinguished scholar enjoying a lively discussion with the chapel's elderly caretaker.

After the meeting Lord Mackintosh commented to the caretaker that he had seemed to get on very well with the professor. "Oh, yes, it was easy," said the old man. "I knew I had no edication, so I just used me brains."

This, surely, is what education is all about!

TUESDAY—AUGUST 7.

I LIKE the story of the man who went into church wearing a bowler hat. A man on duty at the door welcomed him, gave him a hymn book, and said, "Good morning and — er — would you mind removing your hat?" Another man showed him to his seat and said something similar, as did the woman sitting behind him.

When the vicar went outside after the service to meet his congregation, he shook hands with the man and said how nice it was to see him in church, but it was usual to take off one's hat.

"Oh, I know," was the reply, "but I've been coming here for six months and it's the first time anyone has spoken to me."

It's only a story, of course, and unlikely to be entirely true, but it's a reminder that it's only too easy to ignore a stranger . . .

THE FRIENDSHIP BOOK

"WHAT do you call a rabbit with sunstroke, Mr Gay?" Billy, my young neighbour, called out as he paused at the gate the other day.

"No, I don't know that one," I replied.

"A hot cross bun, of course!" said Billy, running off merrily.

PATRICIA McGAVOCK wrote this moving poem about blindness and how unshakeable faith sheds light in a life that could otherwise be one of never-ending darkness:

Would I could see the beauty of the flowers
  Whose sweet perfume pervades the Summer air,
The grass so soft beneath my faltering footsteps,
  That thing called light I'm told is everywhere.

Then I could see the trees in Autumn glory,
  The little birds that flutter to and fro;
The colours of the rainbow, sunset glowing;
  The changing seasons as they come and go.

But I am blind and cannot see such beauty,
  No moon or stars illumine my long night,
No dawn of day or sunrise in the morning
  Can share with me the wonder of their light.

Yet I am glad, when each new dawn comes breaking,
  To feel the morning air, the sun's caress,
To touch the gentle softness of a rosebud,
  And breathe the fragrance of its loveliness.

The scent of rain upon a country footpath,
  Soft music and a voice that sweetly sings,
God's hand in mine as He so gently leads me—
  I need not eyes for all these wondrous things.

THE FRIENDSHIP BOOK

FRIDAY—AUGUST 10.

THE Rev. Clark Poling was a chaplain in the US Army during World War II. He died at the sinking of the *SS Dorchester* in 1943, together with three other chaplains, Jewish, Roman Catholic and Protestant, when they all gave away their life jackets to others.

Clark Poling's father told afterwards of a conversation he had with his son just after he had enlisted. "Dad, I don't want you to pray for my return. Many will not come back, and to ask God for special family favours wouldn't be fair. Just pray that I may have strength and courage, and especially that I shall be patient. And, Dad, pray that I shall be *adequate*."

Clark Poling was more than adequate.

SATURDAY—AUGUST 11.

A CHARITY organised a clothing appeal and people were asked to look out their unwanted garments and leave them on the doorstep to be collected.

Mrs Smith found quite a lot of clothing her family had outgrown, placed it in a bag and left it where it could easily be seen.

Unfortunately the laundryman got there first and the next week the clothes were back again, all neatly washed and ironed — along with a bill for £6.50!

SUNDAY—AUGUST 12.

THIS is a faithful saying, and worthy of all acceptation, that Christ Jesus came into the world to save sinners; of whom I am chief.

Timothy I 1:15

THE FRIENDSHIP BOOK

S HE was a lovely girl with a happy face and she was gazing into a shoe shop window when I saw her.

"There's no use looking at those shoes," remarked her older companion. "You could never wear them."

The girl half turned in her wheelchair and smiled. "Maybe not, but I can enjoy looking at them."

It was just a small incident, yet it seemed to illustrate what the novelist Elizabeth Goudge once described as "courage and proper pride — two of the finest flowers of human character".

These attributes are so necessary to people facing adversity. As more and more handicapped children and adults are now part of life's daily scene, we have the chance to show our respect and admiration for their courage. However, the way we do this is important.

Harriet, the old nurse in Elizabeth Goudge's novel *The Rosemary Tree,* puts it into these words: "It's a poor sort of virtue that has no roots in love. It's why you do or don't do a thing that matters most, in my mind."

Probably Group Captain Cheshire put it even better in his autobiography published several years ago. He wrote: "If I am physically disabled and dependent upon someone else's support, I have a special need to feel that what is being done for me is not out of a sense of duty, or still worse, pity, but purely because I'm me."

I N the great decisions of his life Abraham Lincoln was guided by his unshakeable faith. He expressed what it meant to him in this short sentence:

"Without divine assistance I cannot succeed; with it I cannot fail."

COUNTRY CHARMS

THE FRIENDSHIP BOOK

C OULD we only see the goodness
Of the ones we meet each day,
We would overlook their failures
As we greet them on life's way.

I came across these anonymous lines recently. It is not the greatest of poetry, but it says something of the benefits of tolerance towards others.

There is a nice story that Somerset Maugham told about his mother and father. Mrs Maugham was a charming woman, loved by everybody, while her husband had few obvious gifts and graces. Someone once said to her, "When everyone is in love with you, and when you could have anyone you liked, how can you remain faithful to that ugly little man you married?"

She answered simply, "He never hurts my feelings."

Y OU rarely see nowadays the framed inspirational verses which at one time used to hang in many homes, but one of these I still remember from my youth, probably because I saw it so often. It may be a bit old-fashioned in its wording — but the sentiments are still true:

Did you tackle that trouble that came your way
With resolute heart and cheerful?
Or hide your face from the light of day
With a craven soul and fearful?
Oh, a trouble's a ton or a trouble's an ounce,
Or a trouble is what you make it,
And it isn't the fact that you're hurt that counts
But only — how did you take it?

THE FRIENDSHIP BOOK

THESE lines of encouragement were sent me by Phyllis Birchall. I gladly pass them on:

Remember, there's always a rainbow, wherever a cloud appears, remember there's always tomorrow, although you have doubts and fears. Someone is there to listen, if only you'll stop and pray, someone is close beside you to help you on your way. So if you are one of those people who find life is hard to bear, just stretch out your hand in the darkness — you'll find God waiting there.

THE composing of hymns has usually been inspired by the writer's deepest experiences or else by a direct thought from scripture. The latter was the case with Harriet Auber when she wrote her beautiful Whitsuntide hymn.

She was sitting in her bedroom one Whit Sunday thinking about the sermon she had heard that morning on the coming of the Holy Spirit, when the words of "Our blest Redeemer, e'er he breathed his tender, last farewell" came into her mind. She had neither paper nor pen handy, but being anxious not to forget them, she scratched on her window pane with the diamond in her ring.

After Harriet's death, a dealer tried to buy the pane of glass as an interesting curio, but this was refused. Unfortunately the glass was later cut out and stolen, and has never been seen again. The hymn, however, lives on.

AND he said unto him, Son, thou art ever with me, and all that I have is thine. Luke 15:31

GLORIOUS SUMMER

THE FRIENDSHIP BOOK

HAVE you heard this definition of a procrastinator? It's someone who puts off until tomorrow the things that have already been put off until today!

Often it is the first step that is the hardest to take, but it's worth remembering that each day is precious, and if we can go to bed knowing that we have enjoyed and used it to the best of our ability, then there's nothing to regret.

Every new day brings a fresh opportunity — and we will surely get out of it whatever we put in.

A LOCAL church has many links with the USA, so it was no surprise to see in its recent parish magazine the following extract from St Timothy's in Fort Worth, appropriately entitled "The 23rd Channel":

"The TV is my shepherd, I shall not want. It makes me to lie down on the sofa. It leads me in the paths of sex and violence. Yea, though I walk in the shadow of Christian responsibilities, there will be no interruption, for the TV is with me. Its cable and its remote control, they comfort me. It prepares a commercial before me in the presence of my worldliness. It anoints my head with humanism and consumerism; my coveting runneth over. Surely laziness and superficiality shall follow me all the days of my life, and I shall dwell in the house watching TV forever."

That may be too harsh a criticism of a medium which gives many people a great deal of pleasure. It reminds us, though, that, like many other things, TV is a good servant, but a very poor master.

THE FRIENDSHIP BOOK

WEDNESDAY—AUGUST 22.

WHEN an African has a heavy load to carry, he will often tie it to one end of a pole with a stone of equal weight fastened to the other. Then, with the pole across his shoulder he is able to carry his load in the easiest possible way.

It's the same idea as packing our holiday luggage into two small suitcases to balance one another when we're carrying them, rather than in one large heavy bag that weighs us down.

It works like that in life, too. Many people have found that the best way to cope with their own troubles is to help to carry someone else's as well. By turning their attention to the problems of another person, it becomes much easier to forget their own.

Simple but true!

THURSDAY—AUGUST 23.

THE lovely island of Iona off the west coast of Scotland, warmed by the Gulf Stream and boasting beautiful silvery beaches, has hardly changed in places since St Columba arrived in AD 563 and built a monastery there. He was a peace-loving man whose name means "a dove".

Today, many visitors and pilgrims visit the island and return refreshed by its peace and tranquillity. Here is one of Columba's beautiful prayers which I'd like to share with you:

> *Be thou a bright flame before me,*
> *Be thou a guiding star above me,*
> *Be thou a smooth path below me,*
> *Be thou a kindly shepherd behind me,*
> *Today — tonight — and forever.*

Why not use it as your own prayer today?

FRIDAY—AUGUST 24.

WHAT is the secret of eternal youth? I really don't know what keeps some older people so young at heart except that perhaps faith, hope and a sense of humour may help as, I think, this story of optimism illustrates.

An old angler was sitting patiently in the shade by the river, watching his unmoving line, when a rambler approached him.

"Hello!" said the walker. "How many have you caught today?"

"Well," replied the old gentleman, with a twinkle in his eye, "when I've caught this one — and another — I'll have a couple!"

SATURDAY—AUGUST 25.

AS we enjoy the long, light days and sunshine of Summer, I'd like to share this evocative verse with you:

> The sunshine of a Summer day,
>   A blue and silver sea,
> The wonder of a garden plot—
>   And all of these are free.
> A sunset's splendour, singing birds,
>   The green of fields and trees,
> How strange that there should be no tax
>   On riches such as these!

SUNDAY—AUGUST 26.

VERILY, verily, I say unto you, The hour is coming, and now is, when the dead shall hear the voice of the Son of God: and they that hear shall live.

                                                    John 5:25

PARADISE MEADOW

THE FRIENDSHIP BOOK

J. B. PHILLIPS is well-known as a translator of the New Testament and author of many Christian books. In his autobiography he tells a story of how, as a student, he helped with the Children's Holiday Beach Missions.

At the time he was extremely poor, and unable to pay the modest fees of the mission house party, but he remembered the words of Christ, "Ask and it shall be given you" — and he did just that. Within two minutes he had picked up a valuable sapphire ring, sparkling in the shingle. On his way to the police station, he spotted a notice in the post office window offering £20 reward for the return of the lost ring.

The owner was delighted to get it back and when he was told that Phillips intended giving half the reward to the Mission, he decided to increase the sum offered. All a lucky coincidence? I don't think so.

DOROTHY felt that it simply couldn't be done — there was no place where a suitable room could be rented to teach some underprivileged children.

However, Jean thought differently and even though the room she found was crowded, the neighbourhood that the town thought would be hopeless proved to be far more responsive than anyone expected.

Dorothy couldn't understand it — until Jean's brother Harold showed her a motto. It read: "People who say it cannot be done are interrupted by somebody doing it."

Harold said, "Just stick that in the corner of your looking-glass, and look at it every morning — it may cure you of pessimism yet." It did!

THE FRIENDSHIP BOOK

I LIKE this prayer from an old New England sampler. It's a nice reminder about all those who have brought love into our lives, perhaps over many years, and of how wide a circle it is:

God bless all those that I love;
God bless all those that love me.
God bless all those that love those that I love
And all those that love those that love me.

WHEN something comes along to upset us, it is all too easy to get a bit depressed. Ralph Waldo Emerson must have experienced this for he wrote:

"All my hurts my garden spade can heal. A woodland walk, a quest of river grapes, a mocking thrush, a wild rose or rock-loving columbine, salve my worst wounds."

Like so many others, he had discovered that to spend some time amongst the beauty and peace of Nature, can put everything into perspective again. You don't have to be in the countryside — a few minutes spent walking in a park or working in the garden will do wonders.

AREN'T children delightful? Six-year-old Ben came home from school one day with pink cheeks.

"I think I'm getting married, Mummy," he announced.

"What makes you think that?" replied his mother.

"Well, I was in the playground this afternoon and Emma came and kissed me."

SEPTEMBER

<u>SATURDAY—SEPTEMBER 1.</u>

THERE'S a lot to think about in this poem by
J. M. Robertson:

> *Life can be a journey*
> *With many variations,*
> *A challenge — an adventure,*
> *With changing destinations.*
>
> *It starts at Optimism,*
> *Then moves along the way,*
> *Passing through Confusion,*
> *Delight, and then Dismay.*
>
> *There's the all-important question,*
> *That the cross-roads stop entails —*
> *Take the straight and narrow,*
> *Or wander off the rails?*
>
> *Watch out for the sign-posts,*
> *And study them with care.*
> *Some can lead to Happiness,*
> *Others to Despair.*
>
> *Though no one knows for certain*
> *What lies around the bend,*
> *Always travel hopefully*
> *Until the journey's end.*

<u>SUNDAY—SEPTEMBER 2.</u>

THAT at the name of Jesus every knee should
bow, of things in heaven, and things in earth,
and things under the earth.   Philippians 2:10

MASTERPLAN

Life's a sort of patchwork
Quite haphazard in design,
With odd-shaped, jigsaw sections,
Not easy to define,
But view it from a distant height —
You'll see the pieces match all right!

THE FRIENDSHIP BOOK

THE other day in the High Street, I met a neighbour of ours, a sprightly-looking pensioner, who had just alighted from a bus and was smiling broadly.

"You're looking very pleased with yourself," I remarked.

"I know," was the reply. "A lovely thing has just happened to me, Francis. When I held out my pensioner's pass entitling me to half-fare, the conductor looked at me and then leaned over and whispered, 'You'd better give that back to your mother, love!'"

ONE of the nicest harvest stories I have heard was told by a lady who appeared on a "Songs of Praise" television programme.

Now elderly, she said that she had fostered over 100 children from tiny babies to teenagers and that altogether more than 200 children had been in her care.

When she was only eight, she had decided what her life's work was going to be. Her mother had taken in a two-day-old baby whose mother had died and as the little girl looked into the cradle, she knew that for the rest of her life she wanted to look after orphaned children.

She once told her husband that she had sometimes regretted that she had no children of her own. He had smiled and replied, "God doesn't choose many women to look after 200 children."

"And," she concluded, "I look on those children as my own harvest — the little ones I was lent to love and care for."

K

THE FRIENDSHIP BOOK

ALBERT trims the grass verges along our road, and generally keeps the place tidy. He's a good workman, and the Lady of the House, who appreciates what he does, often takes him out a cup of tea and a biscuit.

One day there was a knock on the door — it was our worthy workman. He had a bunch of sweet peas in one hand, and a box of freshly picked runner beans in the other. "For you," he said to the Lady of the House, smiling. "They're fresh from my garden with thanks for all your kindness."

"But it was nothing!" exclaimed the Lady of the House.

"Nothing?" he repeated slowly. "Well, it depends on how you look at it. You see, *it was more than anyone else did.*"

THE late Dr William Barclay, well-known Biblical scholar, professor, writer and broadcaster, once said, "I sometimes feel that the most dangerous phrases in our vocabulary are those which begin, 'It's not worth . . .' Just think of a few — 'it's not worth starting', 'it's not worth bothering about', 'it's not worth the trouble', 'it's not worth trying'."

Of course there *are* worthless things in life, but I am sure also that we miss many an opportunity of filling in an idle moment, of speaking a friendly word, of doing a kindly deed, of making a special effort, or of putting right some little wrong, because we feel it is not worthwhile.

When I come to think about it, I feel I am going to have quite an exciting day looking for and doing some of the things which yesterday I thought weren't worth while. How about you?

THE FRIENDSHIP BOOK

HERE are some encouraging words written by Hazel Aitken of Glasgow:

Perhaps you feel you've lived in vain,
That you have failed somehow —
But if you've touched one human heart
Or kept one solemn vow,
Or brought to one sad stricken soul
The hope to live again,
Why, then, no matter how you feel,
You haven't lived in vain.

THE Derbyshire town of Wirksworth still observes the lovely old ceremony of Clypping the Church which takes place on the Sunday following the 8th September.

The local people come together to join in clipping or embracing their parish church by holding hands and completely circling the building to express the affection and gratitude they feel towards their House of God.

What comfortable and reassuring things circles can be, whether they be wedding rings symbolising love and faithfulness in marriage, the security of the family circle, a circle of close and trusted friends, or even our sewing or photographic circle!

Let's make time today to be thankful for our own most valued circle.

BLESSED are the pure in heart: for they shall see God.
Matthew 5:8

THE FRIENDSHIP BOOK

IT was harvest time, but when the minister called on a local farmer he was met with a lot of grumbles. The farmer made it clear that he didn't think he had anything to thank God for.

The minister listened quietly and then went away. The next day he went round borrowing plates here and there until he had collected 365. He took them to the farm and arranged them around the kitchen. When the farmer came in from the fields he was amazed at the huge display.

"Yes," said the minister, "there are a lot of plates, aren't there? In fact, there's one for each dinner you have eaten during the past year."

It was his way of showing the farmer that he did indeed have much to be grateful for.

HAVE you heard of the "plus people" and the "minus folk"? The "plus people" make you feel happier for having met them. They shine with cheerfulness — not because they are wealthy, or particularly healthy and wise, but simply because they have acquired a true appreciation of life's sweet gifts.

And the "minus" folk? They are the ones who are always grumbling, never satisfied. They depress themselves — and everyone they meet.

In her novel "The Morning Will Come", Naomi Jacobs has a character, Isaac the father, who comments: "No matter whether you are German, English or Jew — so long as you are good. Not long-faced, miserable narrow-minded good, but cultivating that essential goodness which brings happiness, laughter, light hearts and the real joy of living."

WEDNESDAY—SEPTEMBER 12.

BESSIE loved her Bible, even though she was blind, and she learned to "read" it, a chapter a day, by touching the embossed letters in her Braille edition.

Then she had a stroke which took all the feeling out of her fingers. It seemed like a tragedy. With tears in her eyes she picked up the Bible to say farewell to a book she thought she would never be able to read again — and as she kissed it, she realised that even though her fingers might be paralysed, her lips certainly were not! And so Bessie learned to read her Bible with her lips, kissing the words she loved.

THURSDAY—SEPTEMBER 13.

TWO men were walking down a country lane, deep in discussion. They decided to take a short cut through a field of cattle — and they forgot to shut the gate.

Luckily, no harm was done because one of them remembered and ran back to close it before any of the animals could escape. He said he had recalled what an old gentleman had said to him many years before: "As you travel down life's pathway, remember to close the gates behind you."

What he meant, of course, is that life is never straightforward. We make mistakes and experience problems and heartache, and we're bound to meet those who seem intent on making life difficult for us, but we shouldn't allow these things to master us. Once we have done all we can to put things right, we should close the gate on it and put the incident behind us.

It was Socrates who said: "Remember that no human condition is ever permanent. Thus you will not be overjoyed in good fortune, nor too sorrowful in misfortune."

FRIDAY—SEPTEMBER 14.

FOUR-YEAR-OLD Catherine has a sensitive nature, but her mother is bringing her up very sensibly to face up to her fears.

When they called on us recently, the sky was clouding over rapidly, and it seemed very likely that we would have a storm before long. Indeed, it soon began to rain heavily and we could hear thunder rumbling in the distance.

However, little Catherine was quite cheerful about it. "Don't be frightened, Uncle Francis," she said, snuggling up to me. "It's only God moving his furniture about."

SATURDAY—SEPTEMBER 15.

I DON'T know who wrote this verse which was printed in a church magazine, but it's a nice reminder of the many people close at hand who help to make life easier for us:

Thank you, God, for little things
*   That often come our way,*
The things we take for granted,
*   But don't mention when we pray,*
The unexpected courtesy,
*   The thoughtful, kindly deed,*
A hand reached out to help us
*   In the time of sudden need.*
Oh, make us more aware, dear God,
*   Of little daily graces,*
That come to us with "sweet surprise"
*   From never-dreamed-of places.*

SUNDAY—SEPTEMBER 16.

WHEREFORE is light given to him that is in misery, and life unto the bitter in soul.   Job 3:20

MONDAY—SEPTEMBER 17.

"I REMEMBER a parishioner at a previous church," a vicar once told his congregation, "who loved inviting people to dinner parties. She was a superb cook who planned impressive meals with meticulous care. It saddened her, however, that she never received any invitations in return."

He went on, "Then, one day, someone told her why. Her friends were afraid that they would not be able to reach her very high standards so they were too nervous to ask her. She decided to try less hard to impress, and return invitations soon followed."

"You see," said the vicar, "it is good to be good, but do not try to be *too* good!"

TUESDAY—SEPTEMBER 18.

IT is many years since Goethe wrote these "requisites for contented living" in the 18th century, but they are by no means out of date and can be just as useful a model for us today:

Health enough to make work a pleasure.

Wealth enough to support your needs.

Strength enough to do battle with difficulties and forsake them.

Grace enough to confess your sins and overcome them.

Patience enough to toil until some good is accomplished.

Charity enough to see some good in your neighbour.

Love enough to move you to be helpful and useful to others.

Faith enough to make real the things of God.

Hope enough to remove all anxious fears concerning the future.

AUTUMN'S COMING

THE FRIENDSHIP BOOK

MYRTLE must be one of the oldest flowers. A legend tells us that when Adam and Eve were turned out of the Garden of Eden, they were allowed to choose something as a memento and they took a sprig of myrtle.

It was first used in bridal wreaths in Old Testament times when the Jews were in exile in Babylon, but it was the Roman bridegroom who decked himself with it on his wedding day. Much later, a lady would often place a sprig in her Prayer Book between the pages of the marriage service. When she went to bed, she placed it underneath her pillow and if it had disappeared the next morning, it was a happy omen for the future.

So, with its fragrant white flowers and associations with "true love", it is not surprising that modern brides like to include this lovely flower in their wedding bouquet.

GRANDMA had had a trying day. She had met nothing but capable and talented ladies who seemed to have the most interesting careers, ran perfect households and enjoyed exciting social lives. She came home feeling quite inferior.

Eight-year-old Nigel sensed she was feeling "down". Giving her a big hug, he said, "Never mind, Grandma, you're ever so nice — and you make lovely potted meat!"

Oh, how that hug helped! It doesn't take much to give someone a bit of a "lift", does it? If you want to help somebody to climb a hill, you do not stand below and push — you go first and stretch out a helping hand.

THE FRIENDSHIP BOOK

THERE is much wisdom in these lines from an ancient Chinese poet, whose name, alas, is unknown:

If you are thinking a year ahead, sow seed.
If you are thinking ten years ahead, plant a tree.
If you are thinking 100 years ahead, educate the people.
By sowing seed once, you will harvest once.
By planting a tree, you will harvest tenfold.
By educating the people, you will harvest one hundredfold.

OUR friend Lilian had been ill for a time. Then, although recovering, she was deeply depressed and nothing seemed to cheer her up.

After a rummage in our attic, the Lady of the House announced that she was going to visit Lilian, and she was taking a parcel with her.

"Just some old photos," she explained. "They were taken on outings Lilian and I went on when we were young."

Apparently it was a nostalgic afternoon, and in no time, Lilian was chuckling. "Did I really wear that awful hat? Isn't it ridiculous?" she exclaimed at one point. Then she continued, "You know, I'm actually laughing at myself! I must be feeling better . . ."

The medicine had been effective!

THEN Peter said, Silver and gold have I none; but such as I have give I thee: In the name of Jesus Christ of Nazareth rise up and walk.   Acts 3:6

MONDAY—SEPTEMBER 24.

PRESIDENT HARRY S. TRUMAN was well known for his saying, "If you can't stand the heat, keep out of the kitchen", meaning that if battles and pressures are not for you, then do your best to avoid them.

What a pity, though, that this phrase became synonymous with one of the most comfortable parts of the home, the place where family meals are prepared, where children run home from school to their mother, have grazed knees bandaged, and where many a problem is sorted out over a cup of coffee.

I came across this "Recipe for a Happy Kitchen" quite recently:

A measure of goodwill;

A full cup of understanding:

Mix with joy and add plenty of love.

What a good recipe it is — and for every part of your home, too!

TUESDAY—SEPTEMBER 25.

THEY had planned a day at the seaside and he was downstairs, ready and waiting, whilst she was finishing her hair and "putting on her face". "If you don't hurry we shall miss the train," he called.

At last she was ready and they arrived on the station platform, just in time to see the train moving out.

In stony silence they sat on a bench, one at each end. He was the first to come round. He moved closer, put his arm round her, and said, "I still love you although there is snow in your hair."

"Well," she replied, melting, "there is Summer in my heart."

"Yes," he said, "but if there had been Spring in your feet, we wouldn't have missed that train!"

THE FRIENDSHIP BOOK

"WHO is the poorest man in the world?" John D. Rockefeller asked a class of divinity students. They looked at one another and didn't know the answer, so he told them. "The poorest man of all is the man who has nothing but money."

Rockefeller was a multi-millionaire so he knew what he was talking about. Other wealthy men have expressed the same thought. Often their chief pleasure lies in giving away as much of their money as they possibly can.

HAVE you ever thought of making a collection of cartoons? They can be such a tonic.

Amongst my "gems" are several yellowed with age. A small one, culled from a church magazine, depicts two newcomers to Paradise. They are standing on a cloud, looking in dismay at a large crowd some distance away. One of the newcomers is exclaiming, "This is terrible! I don't know anybody . . ."

It reminds me of this verse on a similar theme:

I dreamt Death came the other night,
  And Heaven's Gate swung wide,
An angel with a halo bright
  Ushered me inside.
And there, to my astonishment,
  Were folks I'd judged and labelled,
As "quite unfit" and "of little worth".
  And "spiritually disabled".
Indignant words rose to my lips
  But never were set free,
For every face showed stunned surprise—
  No one expected me!

FRIDAY—SEPTEMBER 28.

DO you ever have difficulty in understanding the Bible? I suppose that most of us, if we are honest with ourselves, would have to admit that there are some parts we find hard to comprehend or accept.

A lady with just such problems once found herself at a dinner sitting next to Dr Joseph Parker, an outstanding preacher of the 19th century. So she aired her difficulties with him.

They happened to be eating fish at the time, and Dr Parker asked her, "What do you do with the bones in your fish?"

"Why, I leave them on the edge of the plate!" was the surprised reply.

"Well, do the same with the Bible," said Joseph Parker. "Eat the fish, and leave the bones!"

Wise words from a great man.

SATURDAY—SEPTEMBER 29.

I WAS reading recently about some of the many penfriend clubs which link people across the world through the exchange of letters between correspondents who would otherwise be complete strangers.

The motto of one of the clubs particularly impressed me. It has something to say to all of us, whether we belong to such a club or not. It is, "There are no strangers — just friends who have never met."

SUNDAY—SEPTEMBER 30.

BUT whosoever drinketh of the water that I shall give him shall never thirst; but the water that I shall give him shall be in him a well of water springing up into everlasting life.   John 4:14

OCTOBER

OCTOBER can be a lovely month. The ground is covered with colourful leaves, but there is a hint of Winter to come. Sometimes we dread its coming, although it has its joy, too — cosy fires and the beauty of occasional sunshine.

The beauty of the changing seasons is well captured in this little poem I once saw in an old gardening book:

Golden October, your beautiful leaves now turn,
Sombre November, we cheerful fires burn.
We will not be sad that Summer days are gone
And birds now seldom sing.
We'll smile through frozen Winter
And look towards the Spring.

IT'S always a pleasure to see my old friend Mary. She usually has something interesting to show me and on my last visit she shared another entry in her notebook — the one she calls her "Words of Wisdom":

"If we can only keep our hearts young, we shall never really grow old. Your forehead may become wrinkled, but try to keep the wrinkles out of your heart. Smooth away all the unkind thoughts and feelings that leave tell-tale lines on your face and do not allow the worries to drive out all the good there is in you. Try to soar above your annoyances; if you continually carry them with you, you will grow old before your time — and disagreeable, too."

As the Chinese proverb says, "It is not how old you are that matters, but how you are old."

THE FRIENDSHIP BOOK

A FRIEND told me that she heard her seven-year-old daughter saying her prayers one night. She said, "Bless Mummy and Daddy and all my friends, and please make three sevens twenty three."

Next morning her mother confessed to having overheard her.

"Why do you want three sevens to make twenty three?" she asked.

"Because that's what I put in my tables test at school," her daughter replied.

WHEN we have made a special effort to do something really well, it is nice to be appreciated. It gives a pleasant glow of satisfaction when our home-made jam or biscuits are the first to be bought at the bring-and-buy stall, or if our advice is sought about the care of house plants or a childish ailment.

People have always liked to leave their trademark. When stone masons had finished a piece of work in a cathedral, they always carved their own special mark on it. Likewise, for 600 years, gold and silver objects have been hallmarked to ensure uniform quality and to prevent fraud. Originally the maker stamped an emblem on his work such as a bird or a cross, but that was when few people could read. Nowadays the maker's initials are used and from them an expert can tell the date and maker of any piece he examines.

We may think we have no extraordinary talents, but we can each leave a trademark that singles us out as unique. How do we do it? Simply by being ourselves.

K

IN the remote country areas of India, lighting is still by simple oil lamps. In one village temple there hangs from the ceiling a great brass structure with numerous places into which small oil lamps will fit. There are no lamps in the structure itself, so the temple is in darkness until the people come in to worship, each family with its little lamp to guide them along the dark roads.

Entering the temple, they put their lamps into a place in the great brass fitting, and so, gradually, the temple grows brighter until, when all the places are occupied, the interior is a blaze of light.

Yes, it is the people themselves who bring the light to the temple. If they ignored their temple, there would be no light and no worship — only utter darkness.

THOUSANDS of people have found help in the sermons and inspirational books of the American preacher and writer, Dr Emmet Fox. I find comfort and hope, not only for myself but for the whole world, in these words of his:

There is no difficulty that enough love will not conquer,
No disease that enough love will not heal,
No door that enough love will not open,
No gulf that enough love will not bridge,
No sin that enough love will not redeem.

JESUS answered and said unto him, Verily, verily, I say unto thee, Except a man be born again, he cannot see the kingdom of God.   John 3:3

L

THE FRIENDSHIP BOOK

DOUGLAS is a Down's Syndrome youngster who loves dancing. He is a member of the display team with his dancing school, and sometimes gives solo performances.

For someone who was unable to walk until he was almost five, that is no mean achievement. The greatest highlight for Douglas came one day when he went to London to watch the famous Wayne Sleep give a dancing display. Afterwards, Douglas was introduced to his hero and showed him a photograph of himself dancing.

Wayne Sleep, who knew only too well of the struggles that Down's Syndrome youngsters have, complimented Douglas on his abilities, and asked, "Will you autograph your picture for me, please? I'd love to keep it."

What better compliment could Douglas have received?

IT always makes me very sorry when people moan and pull a long face as Autumn approaches. Yes, in some ways it is sad when we see the flowers fading, leaves falling and the daylight fading earlier every afternoon.

But, think of the compensations! There will be more time to spend indoors when we can settle down with a really long book, pick up a forgotten piece of embroidery or neglected correspondence, perhaps take up a new hobby or attend an evening class.

So let's be positive about the darker days and see what we can find to increase our enjoyment during them — and perhaps someone else's as well. Life is usually what *we* make of it, after all.

THE FRIENDSHIP BOOK

*H*OW *beautiful, how wonderful*
If, for a little bit
I'd nothing all day long to do
But sit and sit and sit.
No chores at all, no pots to wash,
And yet I wonder if
A week of such rare luxury
Would simply bore me stiff!

"*O*NCE upon a time there were four little rabbits and their names were Flopsy, Mopsy, Cottontail and Peter . . ."

So began Beatrix Potter's first delightfully illustrated children's book, "Peter Rabbit" which was published in 1901. She was a shy and solitary person who found her talent when she began writing letters to the family of her former governess, decorating the pages with pictures of animal characters. It occurred to her then that if the Moore children enjoyed her stories, probably other children would, too, and she decided to publish "Peter Rabbit." It was an immediate success and in the next 13 years was followed by "Squirrel Nutkin", "Mrs Tiggy-Winkle", "Jemima Puddle-Duck" and a host of other tales.

Quite late in life, Beatrix met and married a country solicitor and settled in the Lake District. There she became interested in sheep-breeding and her writing came to an end. Perhaps the happiness of marriage fulfilled all her needs and she no longer needed to create a fantasy world. Nevertheless, those few creative years introduced many children to a world of magic, and still continue to delight and enthral.

HOMEWARD BO

HAVE you ever tried the Gospel of Smiles? A smile is a sunbeam of the soul which lights up the eye and transfigures the face. It might be easier to frown, but frowns give no light or joy.

A smile can scatter gloom and silver-line a cloud. It costs little, but counts for such a lot. In fact, someone has remarked "a smile costs less than electricity — and gives more light."

Now, that's something to smile about, isn't it?

CANON SUBIRE BISWAS, an Indian clergyman from Calcutta, was in hospital recovering from a serious heart attack. From his window he could see the busy world outside — buses, cars, workmen, gardeners, ambulance men. At first he felt depressed. They were all living busy, useful lives while his own seemed now to have little purpose.

Then he realised there was something he *could* do: he could pray for all those he watched from his window. Indeed, as he got stronger he was able to set down some of those prayers in writing. The result was a little booklet, "Lord, let me share", which, through the Church Missionary Society, has gone round the world and been an inspiration to thousands.

What I like best about this story is that we can all do as Canon Biswas did — we can all pray for others and, in so doing, play our part in their lives. A wonderful thought, isn't it?

FEAR not, little flock; for it is your Father's good pleasure to give you the kingdom.   Luke 12:32

THE FRIENDSHIP BOOK

THE Lady of the House and I always looked forward to visits from Miss Brown, not just because she always brought some delicious home-made toffee, but because she was such a good companion.

Getting on in years, unmarried and with a lovely sense of fun, she made it her responsibility to keep in touch with all the families in our street. If there was illness anywhere, or a new baby to be taken out while its mother had a much-needed rest, Miss Brown was there, and she always had a ready word of comfort or encouragement whenever it was needed.

What a lovely gift she possessed — and she used it constantly for the benefit of her neighbours. Truly, as Victor Hugo once said, "To shed joy around, to radiate happiness, to cast light upon dark days, is not this to render a service?"

AN understanding of children is a marvellous thing. One Autumn afternoon, leaves were falling thick and fast in a country garden. Mr Roberts was busy tying up some chrysanthemums. His son Hamish stood watching, hands in pockets, and not doing anything to help.

"Hamish," called his father, "what about getting these leaves raked up?"

"I'm too tired," replied Hamish, "and besides, I've got a blistered heel."

His father carried on speaking as if his son hadn't said anything. "And when you've raked up the leaves, you can make a bonfire and jump over it."

Hamish sprang into action. "Where's the rake?" he cried with sudden enthusiasm and a miraculously cured foot!

D O you collect recipes? Here is one with a difference, sent to me by J.M. Robertson, of Edinburgh:

> *Mix a little Kindness,*
> *With a little bit of Tact,*
> *Then include some Fortitude*
> *To beat each gloomy fact.*
>
> *Spice it with Sincerity,*
> *Then sprinkle it with Hope.*
> *For seasoning, let Reasoning*
> *And Commonsense have scope.*
>
> *Add a dash of Perseverance.*
> *With a pinch of Pluck, combine*
> *A ration of Compassion —*
> *Now the mixture's blending fine.*
>
> *This recipe for living*
> *Is a winner in its way.*
> *Stir it with some Spirit,*
> *And serve it every day!*

A FRIEND who is a librarian drew my attention recently to a wayside pulpit notice attached to a little chapel:

When you were christened, your mother brought you here;

When you were married, your partner brought you here;

When you die, your friends will bring you here;

Why not try coming on your own some time?

FRIDAY—OCTOBER 19.

ON our country walks, the Lady of the House and I are always glad if we can be joined by our friend, Fred Armitage. His deep love and knowledge of the countryside make our trips real ventures of discovery as he tells us about the plants, birds and animals.

Once, when we were out with him, we came across a dry-stone wall covered with ancient ivy. He poked the leaves very gently with his stick, and then said, "There's an idea for your 'Friendship Book', Francis."

I suppose I looked a bit puzzled, because he went on, "At one time this wall supported the ivy, but now it's the ivy which is holding the wall up!"

Then, he added quietly, "It's like that with all of us, isn't it? Parents, grandparents, husbands and wives, friends — we all do our bit of holding up and being held up, in turn, don't we?"

SATURDAY—OCTOBER 20.

SOME time ago I came across these challenging lines:

Be thankful —
for the friends who have forgiven you,
for the enemies who keep you cautious,
for the difficulties that make you struggle,
for the emergencies that make you think,
for the hardships that make you strong,
for the disappointments that make you try harder.

SUNDAY—OCTOBER 21.

BUT the fruit of the Spirit is love, joy, peace, longsuffering, gentleness, goodness, faith, meekness, temperance: against such there is no law.

Galatians 5:22-23

THE FRIENDSHIP BOOK

NEXT to the telephone in a Christian bookshop was a card which read: "Many are called, but many others have left their receivers off."

Now there's something to think about today!

HOWARD SPRING, the famous novelist and one-time Methodist preacher, had the gift of portraying compassion and humour in his work. One novel, "Dunkerley's", tells the story of Sir Dan Dunkerley, a publishing tycoon. For all his trappings of wealth, however, he never forgot the less fortunate.

Someone who had experienced disaster in his life — mainly through his own fault — confessed his shortcomings to Sir Dan. The latter looked at him thoughtfully and remarked, "There have probably been some queer patches in most people's lives. But if we are people of any worth at all, we should be fools if we paid much attention to what, after all, are only patches".

Howard Spring knew what he was writing about when it came to "queer patches" of a different kind — the sort that children from poor families knew only too well in the days before the Welfare State. His mother was poor and had to struggle hard to bring up her family after her husband's death. Young Howard struggled, too, both mentally and physically before he became a reporter, on a local paper and then on to one in Manchester.

In his autobiography he wrote: "The divine humanity and human divinity that Jesus taught was no more than that God is love, and that the proof that a man has made this great discovery and entered into the love of God was that he in turn loved those about him!"

THE FRIENDSHIP BOOK

THE famous artist John Constable once said, "There is nothing ugly. I never saw an ugly thing in my life — light and shade and perspective will always make it beautiful."

A great thought from a great painter.

I don't see why resolutions should be confined to the New Year, and my resolution for today is to look for the beauty in the ordinary, the commonplace — and even the ugly!

RARELY a day passes but I hear of some severely handicapped man, woman or child challenging us by their fine example of persistence and courage.

Deaf people have long been encouraged by the work of Jack Ashley M.P. who was totally deaf from 1968. One of his main objectives was always to encourage hearing people to realise just how isolated deaf people can be. He also fought for many other causes including that of Thalidomide children.

People with other handicaps prove their ability to be in "the mainstream of life". Workers at a computer centre have been proved to be more efficient than people with no disabilities, perhaps because they are determined to make the most of their gifts.

Hugh, a young man living in the south of England, with little control over his arms and hands, operates a keyboard with his toes. Another, Alyn, uses a stick between his teeth to type his poems. His studies won him a place at university a few years ago.

The persistence and dogged courage of such people are an inspiration to us all — especially if we feel inclined to complain about a cold in the head or a twinge of rheumatism.

THE FRIENDSHIP BOOK

QUITE by chance I recently came across two separate sayings about growing old — each with words of encouragement for those of us who sometimes feel the years are passing at an alarming rate.

The first is by the French writer, André Maurois: "Growing old is no more than a bad habit which a busy person has no time to form."

The other is of unknown authorship:

> *Age is a quality of mind.*
> *If you have left your dreams behind,*
> *If hope is cold,*
> *If you no longer look ahead,*
> *If your ambitious fires are dead,*
> *Then you are old.*

On that reckoning, none of us *need* be old!

"THERE'S a bear in the garden, Mummy!" announced the little girl. "Oh, you naughty girl," said her mother, "telling such stories! Go upstairs at once and tell God you are sorry for telling lies."

When her daughter returned, her mother asked, "Did you do what I said?"

"Oh, yes," came the reply, "and God said 'Not to worry, I thought it was a bear m'self'."

AND he said to the woman, Thy faith hath saved thee; go in peace.   Luke 7:50

THE FRIENDSHIP BOOK

MONDAY—OCTOBER 29.

DO you remember 1971 when our currency went decimal, and half-crowns, shillings, sixpences and threepenny pieces began to be collectors' items? Not everybody welcomed the new money and some of us still speak of 10p as two bob.

The most amusing argument against decimalisation that I heard was by an elderly neighbour who said to me, "If God had wanted us to go decimal then there would have been *ten* disciples!"

TUESDAY—OCTOBER 30.

DO you feel discouraged? Think nothing you can do will make any difference? Take heart from these words I copied down in my journal many years ago:

"A slender wire can carry a strong current; a small window can let in a lot of light".

WEDNESDAY—OCTOBER 31.

IN a museum at Beijing in China, there are samples of beautiful silken material and gowns reputed to be over 2000 years old. A famous Chinese expert on these matters, Shen Congwen, considers that they are far more beautiful than anything made nowadays. He explains, "In ancient times weaving was done from the heart. In modern times weaving is done for commerce."

Well, of course, modern life and technology catch up with us all inevitably, yet I believe that there are still many things all of us can and must "do from our hearts", from love. Can we look for at least one such thing today — and do it?

NOVEMBER

THURSDAY—NOVEMBER 1.

LUCY, aged five, had upset her mug at breakfast, knocked over the milk jug and spilled marmalade on the new hearth-rug. Exasperated, her mother sent her to bed in disgrace and Lucy cried herself to sleep. Later that day her father found a note scribbled in Lucy's tiny diary: "Today I muss help Mummy."

The next morning we heard a tap on our door and found a red-eyed young mother on the step. The Lady of the House made a cup of coffee and we listened to the sad story of Lucy's punishment.

"I felt so ashamed when I saw that little note," her mother said. "I was cross and irritable yesterday, but I will never do a thing like that again."

There are always two things to consider — what has been done and what was intended.

FRIDAY—NOVEMBER 2.

WHEN my friend Gwen visited the United States this summer, she brought back many presents and interesting souvenirs. Americans are very fond of picnics and barbecues and one of the things that took Gwen's eye was a colourful paper serviette printed with these words:

RECIPE FOR A HAPPY HOME

Combine happy hearts,
Mix with Christian love,
Add the fruits of the Holy Spirit,
Sprinkle with smiles, hugs and kisses,
Bake for a lifetime.

I don't think we could have a better set of ingredients, or a simpler method!

THE FRIENDSHIP BOOK

THE winter of 1899 was a particularly severe one and great sympathy was felt in Britain for the soldiers fighting in the Boer War. One outcome was a huge donation of knitted garments for the troops; socks, balaclavas, gloves and the like, were sent out in shiploads.

What was not realised, of course, was that it was Summertime in South Africa and very hot! Sometimes in our zeal to help, it is easy to overlook the *real* needs of those whose lives we are trying to improve. Assistance to others has to be not only well-meant, but well-judged, too.

SUNDAY—NOVEMBER 4.

AND Jesus increased in wisdom and stature, and in favour with God and man.   Luke 2:52

MONDAY—NOVEMBER 5.

OUR friend Harry has been retired for about a year now and he seems as happy and fulfilled as ever. His garden, his church, his daily walks with his dog, his secretaryship of the neighbourhood retirement club and of numerous other committees of one kind and another keep him fully occupied. Like so many other retired people he often says, "I don't know how I ever found time to work!"

I met him dashing off on some errand or other a day or two ago.

"You still busy, Harry?" I called.

"Busy?" he answered. "I'm as busy as a one-armed bill-sticker in a high wind!"

Well, Harry always was one for the picturesque phrase, but that was certainly a new one to me. And how very apt it is!

TUESDAY—NOVEMBER 6.

SOME time ago I came across these words concerning hope:

Hope looks for the good in people instead of harping on the worst;

Hope opens doors where despair closes them;

Hope discovers what can be done instead of grumbling about what cannot;

Hope draws its power from a deep trust in God and the basic goodness of mankind;

Hope lights a candle, instead of cursing the darkness;

Hope regards problems small or large as opportunities;

Hope pushes ahead when it would be easy to quit;

Hope puts up with modest gains, realising that the longest journey starts with one step;

Hope accepts misunderstandings as the price for serving the greater good of others;

Hope is a good loser because it has the divine assurance of final victory.

WEDNESDAY—NOVEMBER 7.

EMIL METTLER used to keep a restaurant in Petty France, Westminster, where the welcome was always warm and the atmosphere cheerful.

A journalist from the religious press loved to drop in for an occasional meal when reporting meetings at Westminster Chapel, and her favourite restaurateur would never let her leave without slipping her some sweets or fruit to take away.

"Mr Mettler," she said once, "you mustn't do this — you're too kind."

Up went his eyebrows as he smiled gently. "If I am too kind, then pass on some of the kindness to another."

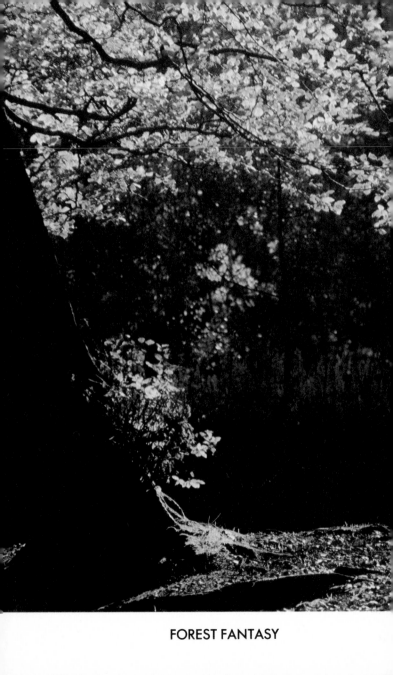

FOREST FANTASY

THE FRIENDSHIP BOOK

ONE of our friends came to spend the weekend with us recently and, while looking at the books in my study, he exclaimed, "How on earth do you find time to read all these?"

I was reminded of those wise words spoken by Francis Bacon: "Some books are to be tasted, others to be swallowed, and some few to be chewed and digested."

I think that says a lot about the wealth of knowledge to be found between the covers of books, don't you?

IN his book "Faith and Inspiration", Ralph Woods tells of a clergyman who found himself in very great demand as a counsellor to people with anxieties and problems — so much so that he found difficulty in coping with them all.

He decided that the next dozen people who came to him he would counsel very briefly and then arrange for them to see him again on a specific date. Unknown to them, the date and the time were the same for everyone.

When the day came and they were all assembled in his study, he came in and told them that he had been unexpectedly called away but would be back in an hour; he suggested that in the meantime they should talk among themselves.

In due course he returned, to find only one man still waiting. He explained to the minister that the others had asked him to remain and tell him that as each had listened to the others' worries, they had realised that their own were really not so bad after all and they had all gone home!

M

THE FRIENDSHIP BOOK

EACH November we wear a poppy in memory of those who lost their lives in two world wars. Since 1921 the British Legion has organised their sale from house to house and in the streets to aid ex-servicemen and their families.

It was a Scots-Canadian doctor, John McRae, who was responsible for the adoption of the poppy as a symbol of remembrance. From the window of the field hospital at Ypres where he was working, he could see red poppies growing in profusion. He remembered the Greek legend that the poppy was created by the god of sleep, and to him they symbolised the everlasting rest of the fallen.

Later he wrote the famous poem "In Flanders Fields" which finishes:

If ye break faith with us who die
We shall not sleep, though poppies grow
In Flanders fields.

In 1918 as he, too, was dying, he asked that poppies should be placed on his own grave.

WHETHER therefore you eat, or drink, or whatsoever ye do, do all to the glory of God.

Corinthians I 10:31

HAVE you heard the story about the church tea party which began without Grace having been said?

The minister thought of a way of putting things right. He stood up at the end and said, "Praise the Lord — and all that is within me!"

THE FRIENDSHIP BOOK

MARGARET WOOD of Rolleston, Burton-on-Trent, sent me these verses which say quite a lot about time and how we sometimes think wrongly that we have "wasted" it:

> *My house was needing cleaning*
> *And I planned to make it shine,*
> *But my neighbour called to say hello,*
> *And we lost all sense of time.*
>
> *The garden looked untidy*
> *So I put my old shoes on,*
> *But the arbour looked so welcoming,*
> *My day was quickly gone.*
>
> *So all my good intentions*
> *Had flown — and I felt sad,*
> *But only for a moment,*
> *For I blessed the joys I'd had.*

BEN LUCAS can be seen with his sandwich-board and Bible in the streets of seaside towns calling upon passers-by to take heed of the Gospel. He's spent many years and considerably more hours, Summer and Winter and in all weathers, proclaiming the message to holidaymakers, residents, business visitors and the like.

Some ignore Ben completely, a few get involved in heated and sometimes hostile argument, others participate in friendly discussion or perhaps listen intently, while a minority poke fun.

"Listen to him!" someone scoffed. "The man's cracked!"

To which another onlooker said quietly, "You'll often see a light peeping through a crack."

THURSDAY—NOVEMBER 15.

DURING a spell of very bad Winter weather, an unemployed man was asked if he would clear a footpath in front of a house. He was quite willing, even though the path was icy and difficult to negotiate. Twice, while he was discussing terms with the householder, he slipped and measured his length.

When he had picked himself up, the man was asked whether his pay should be on the basis of piece work or day work.

"If you don't mind, sir, I reckon we should call it a sliding scale!"

FRIDAY—NOVEMBER 16.

I LIKE these amusing tongue-in-cheek lines about the "peace and quiet" of village life:

This pretty little village, far away from care and strife,
Is just the place for those who wish to lead a quiet life,
For here the peaceful pleasures of the countryside are found.
From early morn to sunset you will hardly hear a sound
But the gobbling of the turkeys and the cackling of the hens
And the bleating of the sheep as they are driven to their pens,
And the braying of the donkey and the barking of the dogs,
And the chirping of the crickets and the croaking of the frogs.
Yes, the dwellers in this village have a very peaceful lot,
For with just a few exceptions it's a quiet little spot.

THE FRIENDSHIP BOOK

"ELECTRIC blankets!" said our old friend Mary contemptuously, when the subject cropped up on a visit which the Lady of the House and I made recently. "Give me my hot water bottle any day. I like the warmth where *I* want it, not where the blanket dictates!"

We all laughed, but thinking about it afterwards, I felt she had a point.

There are a lot of things we have to put up with — we simply have no choice. Isn't it good to think we can still please ourselves about some things — even if it's only where we put the hot water bottle!

BE not overcome of evil, but overcome evil with good.   Romans 12:21

IT was a wise man who said, "Prayer is the key for the morning and the bolt for the evening."

It is something that can so easily be neglected in the course of a busy day. That is when "arrow prayers" are so valuable — the little ones we can offer silently as we, say, wash up at the kitchen sink or dig the garden. Like these ones:

"I'm worried today, Lord. Please be by my side and help me to hold on to your love."

"I'm feeling irritable today, Lord. Help me not to pass it on to others."

"I'm glad to be alive today, Lord. Thank you for my new grandchild and for the sunshine."

It was Baudelaire who said, "The man who says his prayers in the evening is a captain posting his sentries. After that he can sleep."

THE FRIENDSHIP BOOK

JEAN had been having a difficult time, so when her friends invited her to go and stay with them for a few days she packed at once and went. I'm glad to say that she thoroughly enjoyed her days away from home and came back refreshed, and able to face up to her problems more cheerfully.

Of course the company of real friends did her a lot of good, as did the change of scene. But what really turned the tide was a little notice she had seen above a mirror in her friends' house. It read, "You are looking at the face of the person who is chiefly responsible for your happiness."

Her friends were obviously fond of such texts. There was another in the hallway which said, "When one door of happiness closes, another opens, but often we spend so long looking at the closed door that we do not see the one which has been opened for us."

HERBERT SPENCER, the 19th century English philosopher, described in one of his books how, in rolling out sheets of metal, it occasionally happens that a bulge occurs on the surface. He pointed out, "The man who does not know the nature of metal will want to take a sturdy hammer and flatten it out with a few blows."

To do that, however, would crack the sheet. The skilled man would begin to hammer lightly a long way from the bulge and in that way it gradually flattens out.

How eager we are sometimes to strike out at someone else's faults, or at differences of opinion we may have with them! And how much better it would be if we could learn patience and take the gentle way instead.

THE FRIENDSHIP BOOK

"TAPESTRY OF LIFE" is the title of this poem by Margaret Regan:

Dream a little,
Strive a little,
Leave some time for fun.

Pray a little,
Love a little,
Musing in the sun.

Take a little,
Give a little,
Helping everyone.

Cry a little,
Laugh a little,
For battles lost and won.

Work a little,
Rest a little,
When each day is done.

THE well-known evangelist Dr Billy Graham tells an amusing story of an occasion when he arrived for a preaching engagement in a small town he had never visited before.

He had a letter to post, and asked a youngster where the post office was. After getting directions, Dr Graham thanked the lad and told him that if he came to the church that evening, he could hear him telling everyone how to get to heaven.

"I don't think I'll bother," came the reply. "You don't even know the way to the post office!"

SATURDAY—NOVEMBER 24.

I LIKE the story of the lorry which was crawling slowly along the road in thick fog near Hull. The driver was following his mate who had got out to guide him by shining a torch along the edge of the pavement.

When the fog lifted slightly, the driver leaned out of his cabin and shouted, "Well, Fred, we seem to have the right road now! You'd better jump back in."

The figure on the pavement turned, and a surprised voice replied, "But I'm not Fred!"

SUNDAY—NOVEMBER 25.

I AM the door: by me if any man enter in, he shall be saved, and shall go in and out, and find pasture.

John 10:9

MONDAY—NOVEMBER 26.

MANY people have been delighted by the performances of the opera singer, Dame Janet Baker.

In her autobiography, "Full Circle", she tells of her relationship with God, and how this has helped her through an often stressful career. She writes: "When I am singing, regardless of those who taught me, regardless of the musicians surrounding me, I am absolutely alone. There is no-one to get me through the final moment of opening my mouth and doing it except myself — myself and One Other; at times of great distress, suffering or bereavement, I have felt exactly the same. Alone, but alone with God."

The knowledge of being loved and sustained by One who will not fail her has given her the sense of order and purpose in life which we all need.

DINNERTIME

THE FRIENDSHIP BOOK

I FOUND a volume in a secondhand bookshop entitled "A Book of Graces", a collection of verses to be said before meals. Some of them were written long ago by people who did not know where their next meal was coming from, yet they are full of genuine gratitude.

A few weeks after finding this book, I heard a sermon in which the preacher spoke of short graces which could be said, not just before meals, but before play, work, going to the theatre or concert hall before going on holiday and on many other occasions.

What a lot of graces we need today! Our lives are so full of things to be thankful for.

THIS epitaph in Lydford Churchyard made me think — and it also made me smile! :

Here lies in a horizontal position the outside case of
 George Routledge, Watchmaker.
Integrity was the mainspring and prudence the
 regulator of his life;
Humane, generous and liberal,
His hand never stopped till he had relieved distress.

So nicely regulated were his movements that he never
 went wrong, except when set going by
 people who did not know his key.
Even then he was easily set right again.
He had the art of disposing of his time so well,
Till his hours glided away, his pulse stopped beating.

He ran down November 14, 1801, aged 57,
In hopes of being taken in hand by his Maker,
Thoroughly cleaned, repaired, wound up and set
 going in the world to come, when time shall be no
 more.

THE FRIENDSHIP BOOK

WHEN away from home on business recently, I stayed overnight with acquaintances. They were busy folk, and had several callers during the evening, but as time passed, I became more and more puzzled. It would appear that many of them, including the family, knew someone named Janet, for her name cropped up again and again. "I should ask Janet, she'll know what to do," said one. "If Janet said so, then I'm sure it's okay," said another.

Once supper-time came, I had to know who this person was. "Who is Janet?" I asked.

"Janet?" replied my host. "Oh, she's just a neighbour of ours."

"Just a neighbour?" I echoed.

My companion laughed and nodded. "Yes, I can tell you, though, that if you were in trouble, or needed a bit of friendly help or advice, even just someone to talk to, she'd be the first person you'd go to — she'd understand."

Although I have never met Janet, I felt that I knew all that really mattered about her.

DURING the Second World War, a soldier in Field Hospital was visited by a chaplain. He had been badly wounded about the face and had lost a limb.

Very sympathetically, the chaplain said to him, "My dear fellow, you realise this is going to change the colour of your life?"

"Yes, Padre," came the brave reply, "but I shall *choose* the colour."

Courage like that will conquer all that life can throw at us.

DECEMBER

SATURDAY—DECEMBER 1.

HAVE you ever been to a Christingle service? These are held in some parishes as Christmas approaches and they keep alive a very old custom.

Each child is given a specially-decorated orange. This represents the globe and a small candle is inserted into it to symbolise the Light of the World. The fruit is surrounded by a band of red tape or ribbon to signify the blood of Christ. The orange is pierced by four sticks — the four seasons — and on these are placed nuts and fruit to represent the fruits of the earth.

Often, after the children have been given the oranges, every candle is lit, the lights in the church are turned off and the children carry the fruit in a procession, their faces glowing in the candlelight.

It can be a very moving experience for everyone and a wonderful preparation for Christmas.

SUNDAY—DECEMBER 2.

AND ye shall know the truth, and the truth shall make you free.   John 8:32

MONDAY—DECEMBER 3.

A TRAVELLER who visited Warsaw after the last war has described the utter devastation of the city. Yet there were those who conquered despair. One man even put a pot of geraniums outside the ruins of his house.

If sometimes *we* are faced with despair we might well remember that pot of geraniums and thank God for the hope that "springs eternal in the human breast."

THE FRIENDSHIP BOOK

I LIKE the story of the little girl who told her mother she wanted to write a letter to Santa Claus.

"Of course, dear," said her mother. "You want to tell him what you would like for Christmas, then?"

Her daughter shook her head. "I just want to tell him I love him," she replied simply.

AND every hour I say,
Noting my step in bliss,
That I have known no day,
In all my life like this.

Re-reading those lines by a former Poet Laureate, Robert Bridges, makes one realise how rich life would be if we could only adopt his attitude. Briefly, it seems to be — regard each day as a good one and be happy to experience it.

That is easy enough when the sun is shining, the birds are singing and everything is pleasant, but what about the colder, drabber days? Then there are times when we feel off-colour and everything goes wrong.

Worse still when real trouble arrives — illness, death and other traumas such as redundancy and unemployment.

Even Robert Bridges must have felt a bit down-hearted sometimes. He was a doctor who worked in a hospital for poor people long before the days of National Health, and long before he became a well-known poet. It is told how he once commented that the patience and cheerfulness of some of those patients remained in his memory for years. They were grateful for so much, even though they had so little in life, and to many of them, each morning was still regarded as the start of a good day.

THE FRIENDSHIP BOOK

A NTONIO was a hunchback. He was poor, ugly, and of uncertain temper. He used to sit outside the Cathedral of St Mark in Venice, selling plaster statues of the saints, and life was not made any easier by folk who believed the superstition that touching the hump of a hunchback would bring them luck. Many people touched him without asking permission — and this made him very angry.

One day, a charming young girl came across the cathedral square. It was noon, it was hot, and she asked permission to touch Antonio's hump. He was so surprised that he gruffly allowed her to do so.

Some weeks later, the girl came to him again. "What do you want now?" asked Antonio crossly.

"Only to thank you," she replied. "I was in great trouble that day when I came to you, but after I touched you, everything began to go better. It must be wonderful to be able to take away people's troubles just at a touch."

It is recorded that afterwards, Antonio was a changed man. He became gentle and kind, and allowed anyone who wanted to touch him to do so.

No-one ever had need to be afraid of him again.

I NEVER cease to chuckle at the tale of the little boy who was asked to say Grace at Sunday lunch at which special visitors were to be present. Tommy was unsure what to say until his mother suggested that he should repeat what Daddy had said at breakfast.

So, when the moment came, Tommy took a deep breath and said, "Oh, God, we have those horrible people coming for lunch today. Please give me strength!"

THE FRIENDSHIP BOOK

SATURDAY—DECEMBER 8.

IT was a Winter day with a biting wind, but the Lady of the House had made up her mind to go outside and "make the windows sparkle for Christmas". In a very short time, however, she was back in again.

"That didn't take long," I said.

"No, Francis," she replied. "Mrs Percival happened to see me and she said that years ago she had decided that once the weather had turned cold she would give up cleaning outside windows until Easter. 'After all,' Mrs Percival said, 'If I get a chill unnecessarily, then someone is going to have to look after me and that would be most inconsiderate'.

"It made me think," continued the Lady of the House. "So I decided I would be sensible and make a batch of scones instead."

We both agreed that it was a much better idea!

SUNDAY—DECEMBER 9.

FOR as in Adam all die, even so in Christ shall all be made alive.
                                        Corinthians I 15:22

MONDAY—DECEMBER 10.

HERE'S a verse sent to me by Barbara Jemison which I'd like to share with you today:

To help another on life's way,
To smile and chase a frown away,
To hide a fault, reveal the good,
To love my neighbour as I should;
To bring good cheer to one who's sad,
To make some lonely person glad,
To share my joys and blessings too,
This I will try each day to do.

THE FRIENDSHIP BOOK

OUR old friend Mary has been telling us a true story about Emily, a friend of hers, who had served a country chapel as organist for 30 dedicated years. When she announced her retirement, the congregation organised a huge party to express their appreciation of her devotion. She was presented with a carriage clock and many other tokens of gratitude and affection. Several long speeches produced lots of praise and gratitude for her long service, with sincere wishes for her happy and healthy future.

However, in spite of a great deal of effort, no one could be found to replace Emily — so she was persuaded to take up her position once again and she continued to play every Sunday for another 20 years! A wonderful record of service to the church she loved.

JUST before Christmas our neighbour's little girl, Fiona, said excitedly to the Lady of the House when she met her in the street, "Oh, Mrs Gay, I'm going to be an angel in our Christmas activity play at school."

She hadn't got the right word, but I have a feeling that she had the right idea. As we watched the children's Nativity Play in our own church, it seemed to me that the boys and girls were not just playing parts. It was as though they were really there — participating in the actual events of the Christmas story, all those years ago. It truly was an "activity" play for them.

Isn't that how Christmas should be for us all? Not just an event we watch from the outside, but something in which we are actively involved, living the whole wonderful story all over again.

M

TIME UP

HONOR was once travelling by railway during the war years, and had to change trains at Salisbury. She saw her connection already waiting at the far platform, but the station was packed with a seething mass of people. In desperation she cried out, "I'll miss my train!"

Suddenly a brawny sailor appeared. He picked up Honor, hoisted her over his shoulder, shouting, "Make way! This lady has fainted!" Those magic words cleared a way through the crowds in next to no time — and the sailor deposited Honor in a compartment seconds before the train pulled out.

"Thank you," she gasped. "I'd never have made it in time without you."

"That's all right, Miss," he grinned, as he, too, sat down. "Neither would I!"

ONE evening, before the curtains were drawn, I heard a faint tapping at the window. Outside in the darkness, a moth, attracted by the light, was fluttering around, banging against the window in its frantic efforts to get in.

I was reminded then of the legend which says that when all the creatures and living things of the earth were on their way to the manger, the drab, grey little moth stopped to preen itself in an attempt to make itself more beautiful and presentable to this wonderful Babe who was to be King of all the earth.

When at last it arrived at the stable, the door was closed. The radiance from the Halo shone through, and the moth tried frantically to enter, but without success. Ever since, so the legend goes, the moth has fluttered around the light, forever seeking the Christ Child.

SATURDAY—DECEMBER 15.

IN Melbourne Art Gallery, Australia, there is a painting by St. George Hare entitled "The Victory of Faith". Set in Roman times it depicts two Christian girls, one black, the other white, in the ante-room of the arena the night before they are to be thrown to the lions.

On their faces there is no sign of fear — no dread of the morrow, of the lions, of Roman tyranny. Indeed, they are sleeping peacefully! That, implies the artist, is the victory of their faith.

Can we not, too, through faith, sleep in peace?

SUNDAY—DECEMBER 16.

THE fool hath said in his heart, There is no God.
Psalms 14:1

MONDAY—DECEMBER 17.

AN enterprising vicar put a notice above the collection plate. It read, "Be like Scrooge this Christmas!"

"Yes," explained the vicar during his sermon, "I want you all to be like Scrooge this Christmas. Now, you remember what Scrooge was like, don't you?"

The congregation looked puzzled, and at last one spoke up: "Scrooge was stingy and mean; a real skinflint!"

There was a murmur of general agreement which brought a smile to the vicar's face.

"Yes," he said, "but, remember, Scrooge *changed.* He grew to love Christmas and became warm and generous. Let's all change and be like him!"

The collection plate was more full than usual that Christmas.

THE FRIENDSHIP BOOK

IT has been said of Italians, "Their first loyalty is to the family, then to the region they are from, and finally to their country."

It reminds me of what the great Chinese philosopher, Confucius, said long ago, "To put the world in order we must first put the nation in order; to put the nation in order we must put the family in order; to put the family in order, we must cultivate our personal life."

ON the days before Christmas, Santa Claus stood outside a department store in a North London suburb, collecting money for a local old folks' charity. He had a smile and a greeting for every child who passed.

On Christmas Eve, a little girl went up to him. She put some money into his collecting box and then slipped a letter into his pocket.

When he opened it later that evening, Santa found that she had invited him to her family's Christmas Day party.

Next afternoon the phone rang in the little girl's house. It was Santa! He thanked her for asking him but explained why he couldn't come — the reindeer were asleep, tired out after their night's work.

The little girl understood and in an awed voice said thank you to him for her Christmas presents. She could hardly believe it — Santa Claus had telephoned *her*!

What a lovely gesture that was! Of course we can't all be Santa Claus, but, like that anonymous gentleman, we can put the magic ingredients, care and love, into all that we do.

WAITING FOR CHRISTMAS

Listen! Soon we shall hear glad voices
Sing and pray,
In gratitude for joyous
Christmas Day.

THE FRIENDSHIP BOOK

THURSDAY—DECEMBER 20.

IN Canon Charles Raven's "In Praise of Birds", the author tells how he was one of a dispirited battalion who, towards the end of the 1914-1918 War, were tramping back through the ruins of Arras. One night they took shelter in abandoned German quarters. The building had been shelled and was filthy and verminous.

He writes, "Next morning the miracle happened. In a ruined part of the building, two swallows were making a nest. Those birds were angels in disguise. It is a truism that one touch of Nature makes the whole world kin; those blessed birds brought instant relief to the nerves and tempers of the mess. Never was a nest so protected . . . no one could be down-hearted when the early 'stand to' was terminated by the carolling of the cock, and we rushed back to see whether the hen had laid overnight".

It was a sign that, even in that war-torn part of the world where all was misery and degradation, life still went on, and beauty was not so far away as it must have seemed.

FRIDAY—DECEMBER 21.

NO doubt you have heard of Nativity plays which didn't go entirely according to plan.

One small boy in a Worcestershire village was most annoyed at being made the innkeeper when he had wanted to be a wise man and wear a crown. When Joseph knocked at his door, he said, "Come in — there's plenty of room!"

He might have wrecked the whole show, but a quick-witted Joseph looked inside and said, "I'm not taking my wife into a place like that. Come on, Mary, we'll sleep in the stable!"

THE FRIENDSHIP BOOK

PHYLLIS ELLISON of Bolton sends me a few verses from time to time. Here is one that particularly took my fancy:

Is it just coincidence,
That when I wear a smile,
Things seem so much brighter,
Living more worthwhile?
Is it just coincidence,
Or is it really true,
That if you wear a sunny smile,
The whole world smiles with you?

AND she brought forth her firstborn son, and wrapped him in swaddling clothes, and laid him in a manger: because there was no room for them in the inn. — Luke 2:7

I LIKE these opening words of a Christmas prayer: "At this time when the solitary are set in families, when children's children gather under the old roof, and wanderers and exiles think longingly of home . . ."

Yes, Christmas is a time when we all think of home, and most of us try to be there if we can. Charles Dickens put it this way: "And I *do* come home for Christmas. We all do, or we all should. We all come home or ought to come home for a short holiday — the longer the better — from the great boarding school, where we are for ever working at our arithmetical slates, to take and give a rest."

A happy Christmas to you all, too!

TUESDAY—DECEMBER 25.

O NE Christmas morning, an elderly lady was sitting all by herself in her home when the doorbell rang.

Outside was a young man who played the trumpet in the local brass band. He wanted to know if she had any favourite carols he could play for her.

The old lady wasn't really a brass band fan, but she let him play for her all the same and he produced music of such beauty and feeling that she offered him a coin — and was surprised when he said he didn't want anything.

"I just thought it a nice idea to play for someone on this special day," he explained.

That young man knew what the tidings of comfort and joy were all about. By sharing his music with the lonely, he reflected the true kindness and goodwill of the Christmas season.

WEDNESDAY—DECEMBER 26.

D O you know what a sheet-anchor is? It's the second anchor used in an emergency and the very words suggest something solid and reliable. However, sheet-anchors can take many forms as the historian John Richard Green once pointed out. Under the heading "Sheet-Anchors" he wrote:

"What seems to grow fairer to me as life goes by is its love and grace and tenderness; not its wit and cleverness and grandeur of knowledge, grand as knowledge is, but just the laughter of little children and the friendship of friends and the cosy talk by the fireside and the sight of flowers and the sound of music".

These things, too, can be a sheet-anchor, always there, always to be relied upon, to see you through the storms of life.

A YOUNG schoolteacher was travelling through a beautiful part of Somerset. She had been ill and was just beginning to get her strength back.

In her head, day after day, an old Greek melody kept repeating itself. It would make a wonderful tune for a hymn, she thought.

At last, she took out pencil and paper and began to write. The words she jotted down was the first verse of a hymn which has been dear to young and old over the past 150 years.

I think when I read that sweet story of old
When Jesus was here among men,
How he called little children as lambs to his fold,
I should like to have been with him then . . .

The young teacher was Jemima Thompson, and her hymn was first sung in the Sunday school where her father was superintendent. When he heard it for the first time, he didn't know that his daughter was the composer, but when he found out he was so delighted that, without her knowing, he sent it to a publisher and soon it was being sung in churches everywhere.

B ENJAMIN FRANKLIN, the 18th century American statesman who helped to draft the Declaration of Independence, moved in high places, but he also took a delight in simple things.

He once wrote: "Happiness is less the result of great gifts of fortune which come rarely than the thousand little joys of everyday. It's the everyday things that matter — family ties, friends, books, flowers, food, water, the wind, health, shelter, sleep, the open road, rain in Summer, fire in Winter, dawn, the starry sky, love in youth and memory in old age. Are not these vast commonplaces the very gist of life?"

THE FRIENDSHIP BOOK

THE people of India have many beautiful customs and ceremonies. Here is a marriage blessing I came on recently:

Now for you, there is no rain
For one is shelter to the other.
Now for you, the sun shall not burn
For one is shelter to the other.
Now for you, nothing is hard or bad
For the goodness and badness is taken
By one for the other.

Now for you, there is no night
For one is light to the other.
Now for you, the snow has ended always
For one is protection for the other.
It is that way, from now on, from now on.
Now it is good and there is always food,
And now there is always drink,
And now there is comfort,
Now there is no loneliness.

UNTO him be glory in the church by Christ Jesus throughout all ages, world without end. Amen.

Ephesians 3:21

AT this time of year when we are looking back over the past, and thinking of the future, and perhaps making new resolutions, we might well remember the words of an anonymous writer: "He is happiest who is a miser of good memories and a spendthrift of good deeds."

Where the Photographs Were Taken

WATENDLATH, CUMBRIA — *Always Another Day.*
TOWN HEAD, CUMBRIA — *Hidden Valley.*
BATH ABBEY — *Lighting Our Darkness.*
EDINBURGH CASTLE — *The Message.*
DUDLEY MUSEUM, WEST MIDLANDS — *Good Old Ways.*
BUDE, CORNWALL — *Golden Rest.*
ST DAVID'S CATHEDRAL, PEMBROKESHIRE — *House Of Faith.*

BINTREE MILL, NORFOLK — *A Quiet Corner.*
MARSDEN BAY, TYNE & WEAR — *Perfect Holiday.*
BRODICK CASTLE, ARRAN — *Bright Spring.*
COCKINGTON VILLAGE, DEVON — *Three's Company.*
FALLS OF DOCHART, KILLIN — *Time To Sit And Talk.*
BRAMHAM PARK FAIRGROUND, WEST YORKSHIRE — *The Fun Of The Fair.*

CARDIFF CASTLE — *King Of The Castle.*
BALMERINO, FIFE — *Country Charms.*
CASTLEWELLAN FOREST PARK, CO. DOWN — *Glorious Summer.*

THE MALVERNS — *A Day To Remember.*
WEYMOUTH, DORSET — *Homeward Bound.*
RIVER COLN, BIBURY, GLOUCESTERSHIRE — *Dinnertime.*
BIG BEN, LONDON — *Time Up.*
TEWKESBURY ABBEY, GLOUCESTERSHIRE — *Waiting For Christmas.*

Printed and Published by D. C. THOMSON & CO., LTD.,
185 Fleet Street, London EC4A 2HS.

© D. C. Thomson & Co., Ltd., 1989.

ISBN 0-85116-459-5